READ THIS FIRST

We can't wait for you to get started with our high cocktail recipes but before jumping in please be sure to read the following disclaimer and information carefully.

By using our cocktail recipes you agree to the following terms.

You are 18 years of age or older. This is a publication of freedom of press. We only inform and show how to prepare the cocktails. All recipes are solely meant for individual usage and are at your own risk.

All ingredients in our recipes can be purchased legally in The Netherlands due to a declaration of tolerance. However, altering psychotropic substances is illegal in The Netherlands.

We cannot provide any information on the legal status of an ingredient in your country, so please do not ask us. You accept the responsibility to inform yourself about your local laws. We do not encourage the illegal use of products. We strongly advise you to consult a lawyer, if you have any doubts.

High Cuisine and The Bulldog make no claim that the information and ingredients in the recipes are available, appropriate or legal outside The Netherlands. All information provided by High Cuisine and The Bulldog, through this book, our website, links to or from other websites or by its employees over the phone, email or any other transmission is purely for educational and informational purposes. This should never be interpreted as a recommendation to undertake a specific action. Using the information for illegal activities is at your own risk.

High Cuisine and The Bulldog do not warrant that the information in the book or on the website is up-to-date or accurate. This book may not be accessed, viewed or otherwise received in any country or location in which doing so would, or could be, deemed a violation of any law, community standard or customs regulation. High Cuisine and The Bulldog make no claim that our recipes are suitable for treating any disease, to cure, diagnose an illness or prevent diseases. High Cuisine and The Bulldog do not provide any specific medical advice. Do not use any of our recipes if you have high blood pressure, heart disease, diabetes or any other health problems. Do not use any of the ingredients if you're pregnant, nursing, taking MAO inhibitors, medicines or any other (prescription) drug. Do not drive or operate machinery after using our recipes. If you have any doubts, always ask your doctor's advice. Do not combine the recipes with alcohol.

You're taking full liability for personal injury, damages, punitive measures, lost profit or revenues, loss of use of product or equipment and any loss of property that may result from the purchase, ingestion, use or misuse of any recipe from High Cuisine and The Bulldog. High Cuisine and The Bulldog, its owners, agents, publishers and employees cannot be held responsible for the actions of its customers.

All illustrations, pictures, design, text and logos in this book are protected by copyright. Re-distribution, re-transmission, re-publication, or any commercial use of any of this contents is strictly prohibited without the written permission of High Cuisine, The Bulldog and/or the publisher. All rights reserved.

High Cocktails

Psychoactive Non-Alcoholic Cocktails

Presenting
High Cocktails

7

A Word from the Team

What's Your
Poison?

21

12,000 years of High Drinks

Mixologists
& Recipes

39

Let's Get Down to Drinking

Spirit Plants

119

A Taste of Mind-Altering Plants

Just a Dash

151

Pick-Me-Ups, with a Twist

Too Much of a Good Thing

167

Dosage Do's & Don'ts

The Art & Science of Getting High

179

Entourage Effects, Combinations & Safety

Last Call

191

The Last Word

A Word from the Team

Our eclectic, risk-taking team is based in Amsterdam, and the city's open culture has been the backdrop to everything we have done. It also gave us the means, motive and method with which to push open a door that had long been rusted shut, allowing us to innovate and create exciting new concepts and products.

The High Cuisine team came together thanks to an auspicious encounter between our two amazing chefs, our filmmaker/creative director, a writer/researcher, designer and producer. They got the ball rolling and, like Pied Pipers, enticed the rest of the team to come along.

After a number of successful dining experiences for which the chefs cooked artfully with mind-bending herbs, shepherding diners from one altered state to another, the High Cuisine brand was born. It was a concept begging to be shared with the world, so we did, with a TV series, books, articles published in the New York Times, Variety magazine, The Guardian and a host of Dutch TV and print coverage.

Our first book, Bites, was a culinary explosion featuring delicious psycho-active bite-sized recipes that were simple enough to make yourself. For our second book, we asked ourselves what goes hand-in-hand with delicious snacks? Cocktails, of course. And just like that, High Cocktails came into being.

If only it were that easy. The reality is we've been researching, experimenting and honing the craft of how to work with psycho-active herbs since 2015. We wanted to create alcohol-free drinks that still offered that light-headed feeling. Drink one and get a buzz or drink two or more for a more potent effect.

Amidst our research, we teamed up with Amsterdam's legendary Bulldog coffee shop, cannabis pioneers with over 40 years of experience in the industry. There was an immediate connection. Together we've created two bottled high cocktails that will sell worldwide.

We expanded our High Cuisine network further by collaborating with world-renowned bartenders. Each created mind-altering cocktail recipes in their unique style that not only look like psychedelic masterpieces but are filled with flavour and an array of buzz-tastic sensations.

Combining all this liquid talent has culminated in this High Cocktails book, of which we're very proud. We hope you have as much fun experimenting and sharing these magic potions masquerading as cocktails as we had in inventing them.

High Spirits

Is there any drink more capable of lifting one's spirits than a well-mixed cocktail, expertly created from fresh, authentic ingredients, elegantly blended, poured, garnished and served in a beautiful bar?

Wines and beers have their place, but there's just something about the craft, the ritual and the multi-sensory experience of a classic recipe that elevates and delights, even before the alcohol finds its way to the brain.

We don't claim to have beaten this perfection, but with High Cocktails, we do believe we've matched it while broadening the conception of what a cocktail can be and do.

There's a vast range of feelings, moods and states of mind that are possible when we look beyond alcohol and explore the traditional mind-altering herbs and fungi that grow worldwide.

Eat, Drink & be Merry

Our goal was to take these psychoactive botanicals and incorporate them into delicious, stimulating cocktails - in much the same way we've been using them in our High Cuisine dinners. These led to a TV series and a cookbook, and we thought it was a natural transition to go from food to cocktails.

To do this, we recruited four enthusiastic world-class bartenders in our home town - Amsterdam. We tasked them to work their magic and create herb-laced cocktails that deliver all the pleasure - including mind-stimulating effects - without using alcohol.

Our chefs Noah and Anthony added their creativity to the mix, extending their culinary skills into the cocktail-making arena. The philosophy is the same as our High Cuisine dinners: create an alcohol-free yet still buzz-rich, socially lubricating range of drinks that you can reproduce yourself.

To Each his Own

We hope that you'll find all the cocktails not only beautiful to behold and drink but also make you feel at least a tiny bit euphoric. The experience will be unique to each drinker and depend on many interior and exterior influences ("set & setting") and dosage and the number of drinks consumed.

While there are plenty of circumstances in which you might want to have a drink or two alone - they're great for inner focus, High Cocktails is really about connection, getting together and sharing the experience.

The prosocial qualities of psychoactive herbs have been used for thousands of years by indigenous peoples throughout the world in rituals, initiations and festivities. They are also well documented in contemporary anecdotes and increasingly by scientific research.

Make the '20s roar

Dare we dream of taking cocktails back to their roaring 1920s heyday (but without the Prohibition, bathtub gin and gangsters)? A decade when weary survivors of war and the devastating flu that followed it celebrated the relief and joy to be alive with outrageous, jazz-and-cocktail-fuelled parties.

It is not beyond the realms of possibility that something similar will arise to enliven our version of the 1920s, yet to be defined and named. And there are already surprising social trends that point towards botanical highs rather than alcohol being the fuel.

Psychedelics have never sat more comfortably in mainstream society than today, from research projects at universities to positive reports in mainstream media, glowing testimonies from all walks of life, a stream of documentaries and books, and stock market listings for newly-funded companies looking to capitalise on this new respectability and increasingly demonstrable success.

Similarly, plants are very in vogue; in our diets, for health and wellness, and increasingly in cocktails as part of a 21st-century search for authenticity and the continued rise of alcohol-free, botanically complex drinks.

Fungi Fans

From Vice to Forbes, various media dubbed 2020 the 'Year of the Mushroom', thanks to successful campaigns to decriminalise herbal psychedelics in several US cities, the explosion of university studies and new companies taking advantage of this fresh chapter in plant-human relations.

While not without its own challenges, this popularity is testimony to the increasing recognition and celebration of these ancient allies' role for most of human history. It's an old story, with fresh plot twists yet to come.

Check out our recipes, get your like-minded friends together, compile a cool playlist and who knows, you might even generate your own state of high spirits, that "feeling of lightness, happiness or even euphoria".

We'll drink to that.

The Bulldog

You've probably heard of The Bulldog even if you've never been to Amsterdam. It's the original coffee shop, established in 1975 in the city's Red Light District, and has since transcended its cannabis roots to become an international brand and cultural icon.

The Dutch tolerance for soft drugs has enabled this unique institution - the "Dutch Coffee Shop". But it only came about thanks to the stubbornness and idealism of Bulldog founder Henk de Vries and a handful of fellow maverick entrepreneurs.

By braving regular arrest and never ducking controversy, their civil disobedience forced the government to change the rules. Forty-five years later, they were proven correct as cannabis decriminalisation spread around the planet.

Henk is the last of the old guard founders who built a legitimate international business empire around an illegal product. A man of honour and integrity, cut from the kind of cloth you don't find anymore. It took profound entrepreneurial talent, stubborn persistence, principle and a willingness to break the rules to achieve what he has. He's an icon for all Amsterdammers.

Besides his flagship bar in a former police station and other Amsterdam establishments, there are Bulldog coffee shops in Barcelona and Ibiza, bars in Rome and Aruba, a ski resort in British Columbia, Canada and a resort in Ubud, Bali, plus Bulldog stores in 20 other countries.

(left) Henk de Vries at the original Bulldog

The Next Generation

The Bulldog remains a family business, with three of Henk's four daughters and several other relatives having a role in its operation. While Henk is still at the helm, his youngest daughter Ruby and nephew Michael are charged not just with managing day-to-day operations but keeping the group and business growing in this fast-changing industry.

"My most important task is to ensure we remain true to our beginnings and maintain the company's philosophy," says Ruby. We want to be the 'living room' in which everyone is welcome regardless of colour, creed or place of origin and where they all feel at home while respecting the rules."

It was via Ruby that High Cuisine and The Bulldog came together. "The second the chefs Noah and Tony showed me their 'High Cuisine Bites' book; I loved the concept. I'd never seen anything like it! I immediately knew we were walking the same path."

Michael de Vries holds a key position, managing the Bulldogs food and beverage. "We've always tried to think outside of the box, and working with High Cuisine is an extension of this experimental, pioneering spirit," he says.

As a society, we know how to manage alcohol, what to expect – good and bad," says Ruby. We've had 400 years to educate ourselves about alcohol and only a tenth of that time to figure out cannabis. And now, there is a new learning curve as psychedelic herbs become increasingly mainstream around the world.

> "It's the same with cannabis; if you teach people the amount they can take and what to expect, it generally works out okay."
>
> - Ruby de Vries

"You have to break the rules
to create the rules."

- Henk de Vries

"We've always tried to think outside of the box, and working with High Cuisine is an extension of this experimental, pioneering spirit."

- Michael de Vries

What's your Poison?

12,000 Years of High Drinks

Traditionally, discussions of culture and mind-altering drugs focus on remote peoples and exotic locations.

Many scholars have underlined how unusual Western society has been regarding its low acceptance and use of hallucinogenic substances and mood-altering herbs outside the established commercial and legally restricted range of herbs and fungi.

We are starting to see an upturn in interest and acceptance of the psychedelic experience by academics and the general public, commonly referred to as the Psychedelic Renaissance.

Humans have used mind-altering substances for thousands of years, not just illicitly; ancient societies actually encouraged the consumption of drugs.

Only quite recently have archaeologists begun to study how various mind-altering herbal concoctions have been used in the past across a diverse range of ancient cultures, looking at how and why past civilisations harvested, manufactured, and consumed them.

The emerging research field of Ethnopharmacology looks at the plants and fermented beverages used around the world throughout history to get us 'out of our heads' from many different areas of study: anthropological, ethnological, archaeological, iconographic, chemical, and botanical.

They use various sources and techniques, such as advanced biomolecular procedures, to identify alkaloids and resins on cups, pipes, wine vessels and other artefacts and generally provide information previously invisible to archaeologists.

Psychedelic Renaissance

This cross-cultural, multi-disciplinary approach, combined with rapidly changing public attitudes to psychedelic use, is leading to a re-evaluation of the cultural role of psychoactive substances, showing how they were integral to interpersonal relationships, religious practices, and social cohesion in antiquity.

What's clear is that humans have social and psychological needs for these substances; they may have evolved from being sacred to recreational in more modern times - but who's to say this progression will not reverse? As we come to a fresh appreciation of how widespread consciousness alteration has been and how fundamental this was for individual and social health, connection with the infinite and the self, the question arises: what does this mean for our current fractured, over-medicated societies?

Amazon villager describing his ayahuasca vision (1995)

'Renaissance' means re-birth - to look again at the past and find new meaning in it today. This Psychedelic Renaissance is already provoking a re-evaluation of what we mean by 'medicine', 'the self', the value of indigenous knowledge, and how the ancient and medieval world became the modern world. As these questions gain further traction in society, might this catalyse a fresh look at civilisation, religion and philosophy? Deep questions, but fun to contemplate over a High Cocktail or two.

Fear of a Herbal Planet

Psychedelic experiences are often discussed as if they can be entirely understood in terms of their chemical action in the brain. But their social role varies greatly between cultures, and, conversely, culture has a large effect on hallucinogenic experiences and their significance. As a result, hallucinatory psychoactive substances can only be fully understood by understanding their interaction with social contexts that differ throughout history and across the world.

In Cultures of chemically induced hallucinations, Vaughan Bell notes what a remarkably minor role hallucinogens have had in the social fabric of British society, despite the plants being widespread throughout the country.

Bell identifies the most striking historical absence as the seeming unawareness of the effects of the 'magic mushroom' (Psilocybe semilanceata) until 1799. Before then, it seemed these common fungi were considered uninteresting and inedible. The first known record is an article for The London Medical and Physical Journal by a doctor called to treat a family who had been acting strangely after inadvertently picking the mushrooms for their breakfast stew in London's Green Park.

Surprisingly it was not until 1970 that native psilocybin mushrooms were recorded being intentionally used for their effects, rather than in cases of accidental poisonings.

Secret Herbal Arts

The other hallucinogenic plants native to the British Isles include species from the Solanaceae family (deadly nightshade, mandrake and henbane). They are better described as deliriants rather than psychedelics, as they cause confusion and clouding of consciousness due to their effect on the brain's neurotransmitter system.

Although the plants' medicinal value as a sedative has been known for millennia, the hallucinatory effects have generally been negatively associated mainly with poison, enchantment and witchcraft. These negative social and religious attitudes would have been a good reason to hide, use metaphors and generally keep secret the preparation and use of psychedelic plants.

More recent research is beginning to re-evaluate the importance these plants played in Medieval Christianity, paganism and folk use. They discovered that powerfully psychedelic wines and beers were popular in northern and southern Europe, respectively, from antiquity until the 1500s.

Hash, Gas and Cactus Highs

It wasn't until the Victorian era that drug-induced hallucinations were treated as a source of public curiosity in Europe. The advancement of anaesthesia led to experiments (and parties) with substances like ether and laughing gas. The Romantics discussed their opium-induced visions, and Hashish parlours became popular metropolitan hangouts on both sides of the Atlantic (copying the exotic Orientalism pioneered by the Club des Hashishins in Paris).

The glimmerings of early psychedelic research began as investigators and explorers in the New World took an interest in the local flora. For example, psychologist William James experimented with the peyote cactus, with Aldous Huxley and a bunch of other tweed-jacketed intellectuals pioneering a change in attitudes to psychedelic exploration that is still evolving.

Nevertheless, from the perspective of many other cultures, Britain and the countries they colonised have until recently displayed a lack of cultural interest, if not active hostility, to hallucinogenic substances.

Even 50 years after the colourful and psychedelic-fuelled cultural revolution of the 1960s and amid a so-called Psychedelic Revolution, the dominant narrative being pushed is one of 'potential medicines' to be extracted, patented and dispensed by scientifically trained experts. They will 'keep us safe' by taming the psychedelic experience with carefully dosed, purified substances injected or taken as a pill under the guidance of a trained professional.

The entire Americas (particularly the Amazon) are rich with hallucinogen-using cultures, not least due to the massive and diverse range of psychedelic plants found there. In contrast, many societies have integrated these substances as part of their culture. Pre-Columbian civilisations of Central America used psilocybin mushrooms, morning glory seeds and peyote as central sacraments in their religious practice and based significant aspects of their culture around them, probably for several thousand years.

The Smokers, by Adriaen Brower (c. 1606-1638)

Higher Civilisations

There are only two reasons we in the so-called modern world take drugs, whether herbal or chemical, licit or illicit, and that's to feel normal or get away from normal. If you're ill or in physical pain, you want to get back to your healthy state. For the majority of human history, physical healthcare came in the form of herbs, roots, berries and various psycho-magical practices we lump together under the term 'shamanism'.

But we're also social, emotional creatures with memories; pain and loss are unavoidable parts of life, however prosperous, comfy and civilised we think we are. Even in a healthy state, there will always be times when we want to feel different, not normal. We need to laugh, have fun and socialise, or spend just a few hours entertained by our thoughts and more in tune with the tribe.

For as long as societies have existed, there have been mind-altering drugs (including alcohol) with which we could, for a few hours at a ceremony or feast, feel super-normal, better than normal.

Putting Down Roots

Many animals have these same drives and appear to know which non-nutritional plants to seek out when sick - and to get high (catnip anyone?), as did pre-historic humans, who observed animals closely. It doesn't take a giant leap of cultural evolution to go from nibbling a plant to tossing a bud on some hot coals and inhaling the fumes, or from observing bubbling, fermenting fruit juice in a hollowed-out gourd and drinking the results. And bingo, we had weed and booze (both around 12,000 years ago). Party time for humanity!

Recent archaeological excavations show that the human desire to secure a regular supply of their favourite herbal drinks (beers, wines) was so strong it led to the abandonment of their nomadic hunting and gathering lifestyle and the founding of permanent communities with breweries and wine making facilities.

It happened many times across the Eurasian landmass, from China to India to Europe and North Africa. While the specific drug plants differed, abandoning the nomadic life did not remove our need for drugs. If anything, becoming ever more distant from nature as the centuries rolled by has only increased the need for connection via herbal drugs.

Armed with new data, archaeologists are probing just how these drugs affected early societies and beliefs. Some argue that the impact of these psychoactive substances has been underestimated and that a drug culture was central to rituals in Mesopotamia, Anatolia, Egypt, and the Levant.
Perhaps even to the emergence of religions from India (Soma, Vedic Hinduism) to Iran (Hoarma, Zoroastrianism) and the Middle East (Wine, infused with herbs, in the Abrahamic religions).

Fermented Grapes and Loco Weeds

The vast amount of mosaics, sculptures and ornaments depicting lurid, sexual themes and scenes of drunkenness uncovered by archaeologists at the newly-discovered site of Pompeii blew the minds of straight-laced 19th-century academia. This pornography (shocked Victorians invented a new word for what they found) was largely whisked away to private collections and the vaults of the Vatican and downplayed the more Dionysian aspects of classical life.

Besides sex, another aspect of the god Dionysus has been downplayed: the wild intoxication associated with his worship. Traditionally thought of as referring to drunkenness on alcohol, the ingredients in the wines of antiquity have only recently been scientifically identified. Scholars had been fine just using the generic term 'wine' for what in reality was a wide spectrum of intoxicants, based on fermented fruit juice but containing a lot more. Wines ranged in strength from weak every day thirst-quenchers up to 'drink no more than one glass' Imperial Orgy-strength.

The ancients, it turns out, basically lived as humans have always done: be born, procreate, avoid pain, ill-health and death - and try and have some good times along the way. At each of these life events, drugs were helpful.

There were more gruesome and magical aspects (animal parts, incantations), but let's stick to herb pharmacology. In a pre-pharmacological age, drugs mostly meant 'herbs in wine'; 10% alcohol content in water is ideal for slowly extracting the alkaloids and other active ingredients from the herbs soaking in it and keeping them preserved. But that raises another reason we were so slow to appreciate the scale and the sophistication of herbal lore in the ancient world: until recently, we were taught to believe that herbal medicine was akin to magic: superstitious mumbo jumbo, a placebo at best.

The Psychedelic Chalice

We can now appreciate that many herbs the ancients used were effective, as stated in the old manuscripts, and many pharmaceuticals have been developed from them as a result. It's taking longer for academia to contemplate that besides being very horny, the ancient Mediterraneans were also very psychedelic civilisations.

That's according to authors like Chris Bennett, Thomas Hatsis and Brian Muraresku, with his 2020 bestseller The Immortality Key, brought into the mainstream previously obscure ideas about the vital role that herbal mind-alterants could have played in civilisation.

Muraresku brings together several theories on the psychedelic origins of religion. He suggests that infused wines survived the collapse of the ancient world and catalysed the early Christian church before being given the 'old switcheroo' - substituted with regular wine in the Catholic eucharist. The church then went to extraordinary lengths to cover up its roots in this secret, shamanic and drug-inspired religion, persecuting its practitioners at home and abroad.

Woman on Ayahuasca, Barquina, Amazon (1995)

While previous scholars primarily relied on texts, myths, murals and iconography to speculate on the herbal psychedelic origins of the world's major religions, their previously 'out there' theories have recently been backed up by science.

Wines For All Occasions

At sites all over the ancient world, from Catalonian temples to Viking breweries, molecular analysis of plant residues on artefacts suggests the Greeks, the Romans - the whole classical world - used some pretty potent infused wines and beers; in religious ceremonies, funerals, sleep, pain relief, and a host of other medicinal uses. And judging by the ingredients that have been found for some lavishly intoxicated parties.

One of the most informative sites, thanks to it being so well preserved under the lava at Pompeii, is a Roman 'drugs lab' found on a private home site. In addition to a wine press, threshing floor and wine cellar, there were large vessels containing thick organic deposits. These were identified as infusions of various plants, fruits, nuts, and most significantly, a distinctive mixture of opium, cannabis and two toxic hallucinogens from the nightshade family, white henbane (Hyoscyamus albus) and black nightshade (Solanum nigrum).

Such a potent cocktail of ingredients is evidence the household was making theriac. This medical infusion may also have been the sort of drink used in the Dionysian and potentially other Greek Mysteries (as psychedelic-induced enlightenment ceremonies were called).

The archaeologists note the site was specifically designed to produce drugs, probably a house wine not intended for mass consumption. But they also found molecular proof that these ingredients were commonplace, from the symposium to funeral banquets, as well as for household use.

Strong Wines Were Biblical!

On the south side of the Mediterranean, in ancient Israel, Persia, Egypt and the rest of the known world, "The use of drugs, especially alcohol as a means of inducing or enhancing the prophetic experience is attested to periodically" (Prophets in Islam and Judaism), probably related to their parallel roles as herbalist-medical practitioners.

Besides inhaling intoxicating substances like cannabis and incense, some Old Testament prophets partook in excessive wine drinking as a means of accessing the divine. The Old and New Testaments are filled with drug references once you know what you're looking for. Not just wines and incense mixtures, but anointing oils, weird foods dropped from Heaven, references to cannabis and vision-inducing burning bushes.

There are indications of infused wines and more potent preparations such as the Biblical "strong drink" (Shekar). Jonathan Ott believes this refers to "an inebriating potion, distinct from wine; probably a soporific or visionary vinous infusion, analogous to ancient Greek wines, of one or many psychoactive plants".

The ancient Jews used such preparations for ritual intoxication and for easing pain. According to A Cyclopaedia of Biblical Literature: "The palm wine of the East... is made intoxicating... by an admixture of stupefying ingredients, of which there was an abundance, to help him fall asleep". It was also an ancient custom to give medicated or drugged "wine of the condemned" to blunt the pain of criminals about to be executed.

(right) 12th-century mosaic from the Basilica Cattedrale di Santa Maria Nuova di Monreale, Sicily

Infused wine not only had pain-numbing qualities but was also "quaffed (by the wicked) in the house of their gods", according to Amos in the Old Testament, giving clear indication it was sought after for entheogenic effects as well. Isaiah also refers to "Mixed wine" taken "by lovers of strong drink, with spices of various kinds, to give it a richer flavour and greater potency". Some prophets might have disapproved, but their comments still suggest that such cultic practices were both known and taking place in the region.

So, What's Your Poison?

Today, we tend to use different words to differentiate "medicines," "poisons," and "drugs" – but the histories of these three categories have more in common than we might think. Pharmakon is an ancient Greek term for 'drug' that means both remedy and poison. A couple of thousand years later, the German alchemist Paracelsus went even further: "Poison is in everything," he famously wrote, "and nothing is without poison."

Humans, strange creatures that we are, rather enjoy poisoning ourselves, and cases of mild poisoning are, in fact, prevalent in our culture when you think about it (what else would you call a hangover?).

But the act of taking poisons is surprisingly complex and hard to define. Is a cigarette smoker a poison-taker? What about someone who likes habanero peppers? From one perspective, the answer to both questions is yes: both nicotine and the hot capsaicin in peppers are poisons evolved to deter being eaten, and both can kill you if you take enough of them. But taken in the correct doses, pleasure ensues.

The simultaneous allure and danger of poisons have proven to be an incredibly potent force in the grand sweep of history, says Benjamin Breen in Tropical Transplantations: Drugs, Nature, and Globalization. It led to the fall of empires, the rise of powerful merchant dynasties, and, arguably, essential aspects of modernity – not least the disciplines of biochemistry, pharmacy and toxicology.

From Scapegoat to Change Agent

To understand poisons' historical trajectory, we need to return to what the Greeks meant when they called something a *pharmakon*. The word had its origins in the pre-Classical era in rituals where slaves, prisoners and other outsiders were expelled from a community during the plague or military invasion to appease angry gods.

But by c. 700 BCE, *pharmakon* had developed several meanings subtly connected to this ancient rite of purification, but transposed from the community to the body: it could refer to medicinal drugs, intoxicants, and poisons or venoms, but also referred to dying agents and magical spells or enchantments.

Perhaps the best overall definition is "an agent of change." Whether this change was bad or good is left open to interpretation: in other words, there was no clear way of distinguishing between poisonous, medicinal (or psychotropic) drugs, or indeed between pharmaceuticals of any sort and spells.

Similarly, *medicamenta* (also "drugs," "remedies," sometimes "poisons," "cosmetics," or "dyes") were essential to the lives of the Romans. They were dispensed by a male physician, a *medicus* in Latin, from his armamentarium of drugs derived generally from botanicals, minerals and animal parts. There were also female *obstetrices* ("midwives") who were recognised as professionals in their own right, particularly in terms of knowledge of drugs, medicines such as fertility drugs, and poisons, which they were skilled in administering.

Between them, the two professions dispensed a vast array of curatives, love draughts, suicide potions and beauty elixirs, all of the surviving recipes that sound absolutely disgusting.

But a thousand years later, Arabian alcohol distillation, affordable sugar and herbs from all over the world came together to give us liqueurs, spirits and ultimately, cocktails. Curatives, potions and elixirs would never need to taste like crap again.

Healthcare in a Glass – Apothecaries & Cocktails

In a sense, many of the ingredients we're using here, and even regular cocktails themselves of the late 19th-to early-20th centuries were conceived of and prepared as health tonics and pick-me-ups. Across Europe and North America, cities and towns had apothecaries - providers of front-line healthcare services for the poor - who served health-promoting tinctures, bitters and elixirs in addition to regular pills and powders.

Before the advent of modern medicine, ordinary people had minimal access to qualified doctors, so pharmacists - or apothecaries - acted as local medical providers. At that time, Doctors had pharmacists make their medicine in the form of tinctures, bitters, elixirs and tonics for all kinds of ailments. Some of these recipes were as old as spoken history; when the peasants of Europe were driven off their land and into cities to provide labour for the industrial revolution, they took their herbal lore with them.

The first US apothecary was established in New Orleans in 1816 and prepared homemade tinctures, bitters, and herbal remedies mixed with alcohol for curative benefit for everything from poor digestion to the common cold.

Many of these homemade healing potions were hand-prepared on the spot according to the needs of the individual, containing herbs, flowers, fruits, roots, seeds and bark of different vegetables. Various ingredients were grown in the gardens of the apothecaries to ensure the best freshness and highest potency.

While there was a fine line between folk doctor and purveyor of snake oil, customers trust had to be earned. Many of the remedies were very effective, based on recipes that could be hundreds of years old, brought by immigrants from Europe, Asia and the Caribbean, and blended with native American ingredients and knowledge.

Celebrity Endorsed Coca Tonics

Many of our best-known herb-based aperitifs were developed to prepare the system for incoming food, promoting digestion after eating. Tonic water gets its bitterness from the bark of the cinchona tree, which protects the drinker from contracting malaria. Coca-fortified wines were promoted by 'the Great and the Good', from popes to European royalty, as the energy drinks of their time.

It wasn't until 1906 that the US government stepped in to regulate purity of apothecary-produced curatives by the passing of the Pure Food and Drug Act (later known as the US Food and Drug Administration), which moved alcohol-based cocktails out of the pharmacies and into the bar, where they remained. Around this time, the distinction between herbs, medicines, and drugs was drawn, and laws were enforced to keep them separate. Cannabis went from the most used medicine in the 19th-century cabinet to illegal worldwide; pain-relieving opium tinctures gave way to injected morphine and heroin, and coca was removed from wine and cola tonics to become cocaine.

The precise origin of cocktails is unclear. Traditionally they were a mixture of spirits, sugar, water, and bitters, and by the 1860s, frequently included a liqueur. The first bartenders' guide with cocktail recipes was created in 1862 (How to Mix Drinks; or, The Bon Vivant's Companion, by "Professor" Jerry Thomas). Besides recipes for punches, sours, slings, cobblers, shrubs, toddies, flips, and various other mixed drinks, ten cocktail recipes differentiated themselves from others using bitters in the ingredients.

During Prohibition in the United States (1920–1933), when wine and beer were less available, liquor-based cocktails took their place and were consumed

illegally in speakeasies. The poor quality of the liquor available meant honey, fruit juices, and other flavourings were used to make the booze palatable.

In and Out of Fashion

Perhaps perceived as a throwback to the square '40s and '50s, cocktails became less popular in the tokin' late '60s and through the '70s, until returning briefly in the '80s with vodka often substituting the original gin, sugary pre-mixes and other novelties catering to fashion rather than authenticity.

Neither the Grunge nor the Rave culture of the 1990s did anything to improve the popularity of cocktails. Still, the cultural wheel seemed to come full circle in the 2000s when traditional cocktails began to make a comeback. By the middle of the decade, there was a renaissance of cocktail culture typically referred to as mixology, which draws on traditional cocktails for inspiration and uses novel ingredients and complex flavours.

With great attention placed on using the authentic healing herbs, flowers, and spices in cocktail recipes, traditional apothecary recipes and ingredients are being resurrected, and High Cocktails seen in this context are simply a natural evolution.

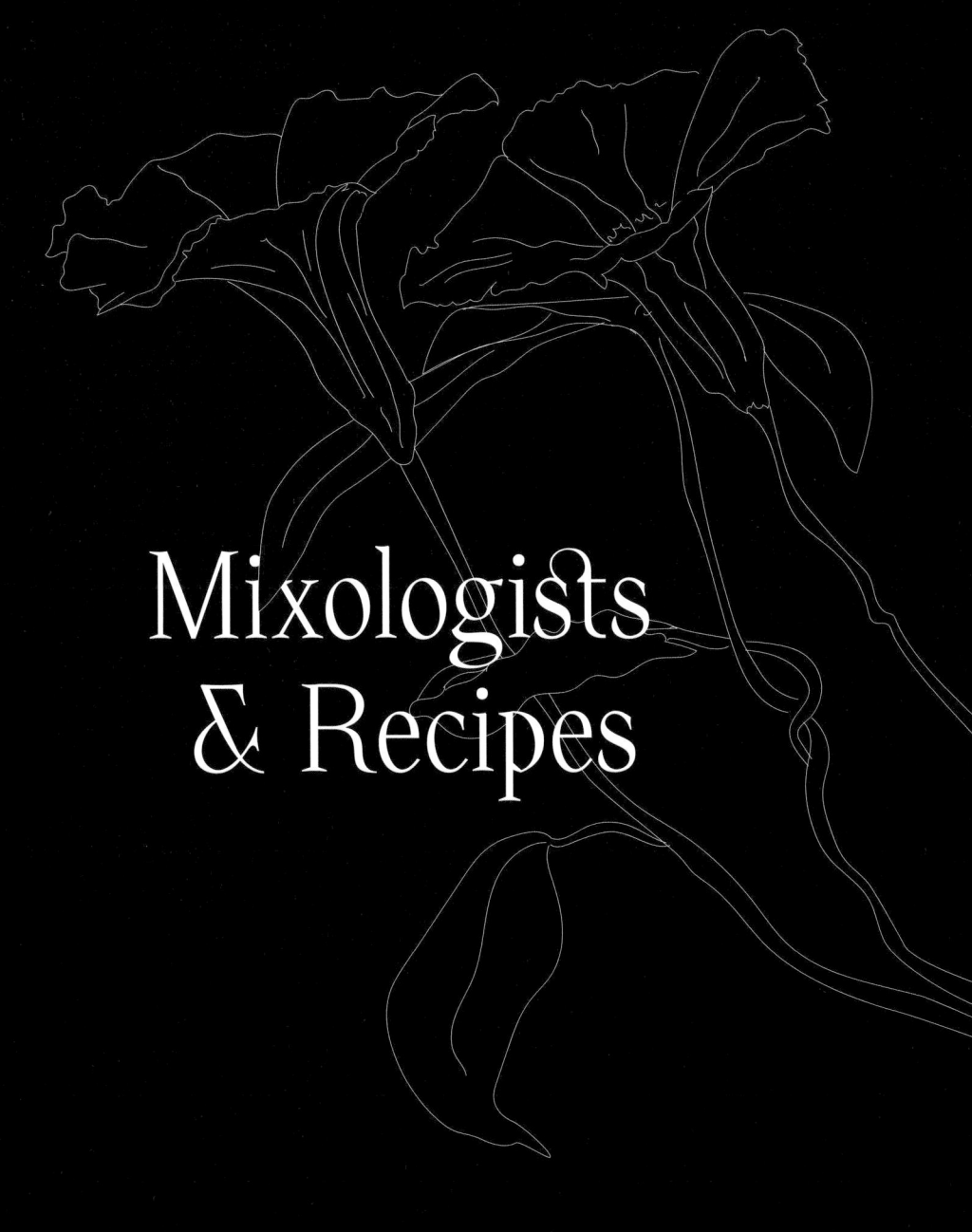

Mixologists & Recipes

Noah Tucker
High Cuisine Chef

44

Anthony Joseph
High Cuisine Chef

46

Joost Jansen
The Alchemist

60

Tess Posthumus
Queen of Cocktails

76

Ben Warren
The Duke

94

Naushad Rahamat
Master Mixer

108

High Cuisine Chefs

"Working alongside world-renowned mixologists was a great experience for us, helping to expand the High Cuisine brand and introduce an exciting new level to cocktail making. The Bulldog has been our partner on this journey, inspiring us with their wealth of knowledge and experience. The merging of these two brands blended beautifully to create this book and recipes."

– Noah Tucker and Anthony Joseph

Noah Tucker grew up in New York in a very diverse and multicultural family. "They were what I call 'zero-fluff, functional Hippies', he laughs. "It wasn't a wild house at all; the general rule was: 'in moderation' – whether junk food, meat, or drugs" – which in his case meant weed and shrooms; "none of the heavy stuff," he emphasizes.

Like his culinary partner Tony, Noah wanted to cook since he was a child, his mom signing him up for classes at places like Tavern on the Green, taking his first real cooking job at 16, in an American bistro in upstate New York.

At 18, his culinary skills upped several notches as he joined the US Navy preparing food for 3500 sailors, working his way up to Captain's Chef.

Noah then spent a year in Japan honing his fish preparation skills before attending the Culinary Institute of America in Hyde Park on a Navy scholarship.

After spending 8 years cooking in leading NYC kitchens, including Michelin-starred establishments, he spent 2 years in California before completing the journey from New Amsterdam to Old Amsterdam in 2008, where he met his culinary partner, Tony. It's fair to say the duo has made their mark on Amsterdam's restaurant scene, consulting to some of the leading Dutch names and starting a string of innovative restaurants and related businesses.

Currently, they own and run several eateries: Yerba, a vegan restaurant, Ladybird, an artisanal southern fried chicken restaurant, and Heritage, a multicultural event and food space.

"Creating high cocktails was a fun project," he says. "It got us to showcase our skills outside of our food comfort zone."

Anthony Joseph
London, England

Anthony Joseph: born and raised in London, got his love of cooking from his mum. "She was a brilliant cook; I loved to watch her, and since the age of 3, that's all I wanted to be."

He completed a traditional 2-year apprenticeship on leaving school at 16, working 4 days a week in kitchens and a day at college.

Since qualifying with a specialism in classical French cooking, he's added influences from Asian and other cuisines, worked in various Michelin-starred restaurants in the posher parts of London under chefs such as Albert Roux and Marco Pierre White.

He worked briefly in the USA and Belgium before moving to Amsterdam in 2004, mainly because he and his wife wanted to start a family and didn't want to raise kids in London. "We'd had enough, moved here and have never looked back."

He had an instant click on meeting Noah in 2008. Together these two influential taste-makers have created many successful restaurants and have consulted for top eateries and upscale hotels throughout Amsterdam.

As for creating high cocktails, Anthony says: "It was an easy transition for us because 1) we'd owned a brunch and cocktail bar, and 2) although our first restaurant, Fraiche, was wine-driven and we never had a cocktail menu, if a guest asked, Noah or I would create something on the spot using the same principles and techniques which we'd apply in food."

Limoncello

Herb	High	Flavour
Kanna	Medium	Sweet, Tangy

Inspiration from a classic Italian aperitif taken to a new dimension by adding the rejuvalac to make it a probiotic gives this another element for a non-alcoholic drink. Replacing the vodka with kratom provides the drink with a unique sensory input. Serve in a medium-tall glass.

Ingredients (serves 1)

100 ml limoncello (see recipe below) · 1 egg white or use aquafaba for a vegan version · fresh lemon peel garnish · dehydrated lemon slice · 1 gr kanna extract · tonic water fever tree elderflower

Limoncello
2 Weeks Ferment Process
1 litre rejuvalac (see recipe below) · 8 lemon rinds · 8 lemons (juiced) · 200 gr sugar

Rejuvalac
2 Weeks Ferment Process
1 litre water · 200 gr barley · 200 gr sugar

Place the limoncello, egg white, and kanna extract into a shaker with four ice cubes, shake vigorously for about fifteen seconds, pour into a frosted glass top with the tonic water and garnish with fresh lemon rind and a dehydrated slice of lemon.

Limoncello
Place the saucepan onto the stove, add the sugar and bring to a boil and take off the stove. Wash and peel the lemons, juice and strain the lemons and place into a clean mason jar with the lemon rind. Pour over the rejuvalac and allow to cool, seal the jar and place in the fridge for two weeks. When the Limoncello is ready, strain into a clean bottle ready for use.

Rejuvelac
Place the barley and sugar into a mason jar, pour over with one litre of cold water, close the jar and store in a cool place for two weeks. When the mix is ready, strain off the barley into a saucepan and set aside.

Clear Pina Colada

Herb	High	Flavour
Cannabis	Medium	Sweet, Fruity

My vision was to create a healthier version of the classic and iconic cocktail while maintaining the authentic flavours and adding a unique twist. It is one of those drinks we all love to sip on while sitting on a golden beach enjoying our holidays. Adding the spice element gives it a Caribbean flavour. Serve in a tall glass.

Ingredients (serves 1)

150 ml pina colada (see recipe below) · coconut and sugar rim · squeeze of fresh lime · 1 ml = (1/2 gr decarboxylated weed (which is approx. 20% THC per 1 ml of oil) · cannabis tincture (cannabis syrup) · fresh diced pineapple garnish

Pina Colada Mix

200 ml coconut water · 350 ml fresh pineapple juice · 100 gr sugar · 250 ml (@ 60° celsius) fresh milk · 1/2 lemon juice · 1/2 tsp speculaas spice

Place the Pina Colada into a shaker with four ice cubes and a squeeze of fresh lime, shake vigorously for about 10 seconds pour into a frosted martini glass garnish with fresh pineapple pieces and THC tincture.

Pina Colada Mix

Place the fresh pineapple juice and coconut water into a clean bowl. Combine the milk, sugar and spice into a small saucepan and bring it up to 60 degrees celsius. Pour the milk mixture into the bowl with the pineapple and coconut water, stir and add the lemon juice. Allow the mixture to sit for thirty minutes; when the mixture is ready, strain through a fine cloth into a clear bowl. The liquid will be crystal clear. Decant the liquid into a clean bottle and refrigerate.

Peanutbutter & Jelly

Herb	High	Flavour
Truffles	Medium	Sweet, Peanutty

The inspiration for this drink came from Choon Leong Lai from Tales & Spirits. This classic American snack was brought to life by pairing the two main components in liquid form, which he brought to our attention whilst experimenting. We liked it so much I told him I would create our own version and give him an inspirational mention for the idea.

Ingredients (serves 1)

150 ml strawberry stock (see recipe below) · 25 ml peanut syrup (see recipe below) · 35 ml sugar syrup · 2 gr truffles · gold leaf · sugar garnish (see recipe below) · fresh strawberry · garnish: flowers

Strawberry Stock
800 gr fresh strawberries · 500 ml water

Peanut Syrup
500 ml water · 200 gr roasted peanuts · 50 gr to puree peanuts

Place the strawberry stock, sugar syrup, peanut syrup and a squeeze of fresh lemon juice into a shaker. Add four ice cubes and shake vigorously for about 10 seconds. Place the fresh strawberry slices, chopped truffle and gold leaf into a frosted old fashioned champagne glass and strain into the glass.

Strawberry Stock
Wash and cut the tops off the strawberries, place them into a saucepan and cover with cold water. Place the saucepan on the stove and bring to a boil; simmer for 25 minutes. When the strawberry liquid is ready, allow it to cool and strain through a fine strainer when ready. Decant the liquid into a clean bottle and set it aside in the fridge for later use.

Peanut Syrup
Place the peanuts, sugar and water into a saucepan and bring to a boil. Simmer for 20 minutes, and when ready, set aside. Remove 150 grams of the peanuts and place the remaining mixture into a blender and blend till smooth. Pass the peanut mixture through a fine strainer decant and set it aside for later use.

Sugar Garnish

Place 200 grams of candy floss sugar into a clean pan and place on low heat. Allow the sugar to completely dissolve, then add your desired amount of food colouring, approximately 3 to 4 drops. Stir the sugar with a metal spoon to incorporate the colouring. When you have your desired colour, pour the sugar onto a non-stick cooking mat to cool slightly. Put on a pair of disposable plastic gloves and pull the sugar to desired shape and size. I use this sugar because it doesn't colour or burn if you use it correctly.

Sour Diesel Ginger

Herb
Sour Diesel Cannabis

High
Medium

Flavour
Spicy, Sour, Sweet

Sour Diesel displays an extremely pungent blend of fuel, skunk, citrus, and spice. It's perhaps the East Coast's most notable claim to cannabis fame. Sour Diesel originated with a guy known as "Weasel" in Staten Island, NY, where it has been grown in mass quantities since the early '90s.

Being an ex-navy New Yorker, this is my personal favourite. A must-have at every bar; this new school classic is my take on the original drink originating from sailors bringing Punches and Grogs ashore. Punch Houses were first established in London in the 1600s. The first record of a 'sour' appears in 1856. Serve in a highball glass.

Ingredients (serves 1)

30 ml organic apple juice / substitute non-alcoholic apple cider · 1 egg or keep it vegan and use Aquafaba · 4 mint leaves on stem · 60 ml artisanal spicy ginger beer · pinch himalayan sea salt · 10 ml yuzu / substitution lemon and lime equal parts · 50 ml infused THC ginger simple syrup (see recipe below) · garnish with your favourite edible flowers

Infused Ginger Cannabis Syrup

250ml agave · 100 gr ginger 5 gr Sour Diesel · 15 ml Vegetable Glycerin

Add all ingredients together. Add eight ice blocks and shake for 30 seconds. Using a strainer, pour into a chilled glass. Pour one shot of tonic in the centre and garnish with edible flowers.

Infused Ginger Cannabis Syrup

Combine 500ml water with 250ml agave and 100 grams sliced, peeled ginger in a small saucepan. Bring to a simmer, stirring until the agave dissolves. Reduce heat to 70-80c and add 5 grams ground decarboxylated Sour Diesel cannabis.

Simmer over low heat for 30 minutes, stirring occasionally. Reduce heat and add 15 ml. of very high-grade vegetable glycerin. You can find this at your local baking store. Cook for 10 more minutes, then remove from heat. You should have 500 gr of syrup. If you have over-reduced, add extra water needed while hot.

Pour syrup into a mason jar through a cheesecloth in a fine strainer to collect the solids. Let cool. Store in refrigerator; shake before serving. The syrup will keep for a couple of weeks. Yields approx. half a litre.

Avocado & White Chocolate

Herb	High	Flavour
Kratom	Medium	Creamy

Inspiration came from a filling that we were using in our artisanal doughnuts at our Fraiche Restaurant. We like combining sweet and savoury to find a balance that matches an excellent profile for a cocktail. The sweetness of the white chocolate balances the fatty notes of the avocado. Adding vanilla and mint tea brings the flavours together with such balance and a hint of nuttiness from the hazelnuts. Serve in a tall glass.

Ingredients (serves 1)

10 ml kratom shot (below)
100 ml avocado cream (below)
30 ml vanilla tea (below)
20 ml hazelnut syrup (below)
4 fresh mint leaves

Avocado Cream
300 ml milk · 1/2 avocado
200 gr white chocolate chips

Kratom Lem Tek
50 gr kratom · 1.5 litres water
2 lemons juiced · 100 ml acid white vinegar

Vanilla And Mint Tea
500 ml water · 50 gr honey
10 gr fresh mint leaves · 1 stick and seeds of split vanilla pod
1 gr green tea leaves

Hazelnut Syrup
200 gr hazelnuts roasted
50 gr hazelnut puree
500 ml water

Place the avocado cream, vanilla tea, hazelnut syrup, fresh mint and Kratom shot in a shaker with six ice cubes, shake vigorously for about fifteen seconds. Strain into a tumbler and garnish with fresh flowers.

Avocado Cream
Cut an avocado in half, peel and chop it, place it in a saucepan, and add white chocolate and milk. Place the pan on the stove and bring to a simmer. Allow simmering until all the chocolate has melted. Place the mixture in a blender and blend till smooth pass through a fine strainer and set aside, and allow it to cool down.

Kratom Lem Tek
Place the kratom powder into a plastic tub add 50ml of vinegar and juice from half a lemon. Add enough water gradually to form a mud like paste making sure all the powder has been incorporated. When this is ready, freeze for 24 hours. Remove the frozen kratom from the tub and place it into a clean pan with 750 ml of water. Simmer the mixture for 1 hour allowing the water to evaporate. When this is ready strain off mixture in a fine strainer or cheese cloth and place in a clean pan, keep the remainder of the residue and add this to a clean pan with 750 ml of water. Add the remainder of the lemon juice and vinegar and allow to simmer for 1 hour.

When this is ready strain off mixture into the first round of kratom liquid and reduce to 100ml this allows for a shot

(contd.)

to contain 5 grams of kratom per 10 ml of liquid. This is the equivalence of a common high.

Vanilla And Mint Tea
Place one gram of green tea leaves in a pan and cover with boiling water; allow to steep for four minutes. When it is ready, pass through a fine strainer and place it in a clean saucepan. Add the rest of the ingredients and set them aside to cool. Pass the tea through a fine sieve and decant set aside for later use.

Hazelnut Syrup
Place the hazelnuts, water and sugar in a saucepan. Place the pan on a stove and bring to a boil; allow to simmer for twenty minutes. Remove one hundred and fifty grams of hazelnuts, put the remaining mix into a blender, and blend until smooth. Pass through a fine strainer decant and set aside to cool.

Joost Jansen
Amsterdam, Netherlands

From an early age, Joost loved combining the fruits and berries that grew around his traditional Dutch family farmhouse into potions, smoothies and juices.

"I loved seeing what happened when I paired them," he says. "I was always looking for the essence of things; how the world works."

This impulse led him to study environmental science at university, where he developed a holistic, whole-systems way of thinking that still informs his life and work as a mixologist.

From the age of 16, he started mixing alcohol into his concoctions. When a friend opened a high-end liquor import business, he had access to quality spirits and transitioned into serious mixing. Besides throwing occasional days-long parties for friends, he worked as a bartender and taught himself mixing skills. Ultimately, he decided to go out independently as a freelance cocktail designer, using the name NixMixMee. That is when the alchemy began.

Based in Amsterdam, he travelled with his work as a bartender/alchemist to Japan, Spain, Mexico, Austria and Germany.

Even with all that experience with fresh fruit and spirits, he confesses, his favourite drink is a glass of water.

"Most of any cocktail is water, so I think it's nice to be able to optimise this key ingredient," he says.

*See our section on Fractal Water.

Flying Carpet

Herb Syrian Rue   **High** Light   **Flavour** Floral, Sour

The base for this cocktail is Syrian Rue (Peganum harmala), the active ingredient originally known as Telepathine, which slowly releases from the seeds into water and glows under UV light, creating a mesmerizing cascade that's psychedelic in its own right. Arabian carpet makers used rue seeds as a red dye and got high from the contact. They felt they were flying.

Ingredients (serves 1)

6 gr Syrian Rue · 55 ml blueberry juice · 15 ml lavender syrup · 10 ml anise syrup · 20 ml blood-orange syrup · Water, fractally imploded or from a sacred source

Crush the Syrian Rue with a mortar and pestle, but save 3-5 seeds per glass. Pour 20 ml hot water over the crushed seeds and add it to the juice. Let it steep for an hour. Strain and discard the pulp. Add the syrups, stir and fill the syringe with the fluid, 20 ml per serving.

Fill the glasses with water, gently stir with a bar spoon and let it settle for a minute. Lower the syringe carefully to the bottom of the glass and gently deliver the fluid to the bottom of the glass. Sprinkle reserved seeds on top. Add some blacklight and gaze at it for at least 5 minutes, then consume.

Tips & Tricks

Syrian Rue is an excellent enhancer of the effects of truffles and thus makes it into a psylohuasca. Don't dose above 2-4 grams of Rue per person. Take care of your diet; Rue is an MAO-inhibitor (see section - Safety: Plants Beat Drugs).

This is a variation of honey mead, but non-alcoholic and probiotic. I used coconut syrup to match the colour of lion's mane mushrooms - and the taste goes well with the other ingredients. As well as tasting great, every ingredient has beneficial effects on one's brain and mood: Nootropic Neurogenesis - The combination of psilocybin and lion's mane makes this drink 2/3rd's of the so-called 'Stammets Stack', fashionable among tuned-in psychonauts looking for a supercharged evolution of micro-dosing. Paul Stammets, the world's leading expert on fantastic fungi, popularised combining (small doses) of these two' shrooms with vitamin B3 (niacin, which increases blood flow to the brain).

This virtuous triple-whammy is said to boost new nerve growth, creativity, hearing and vision, and generally keep your brain in tip-top condition. Enhance these effects by making your own energised water with Celtic-, Himalayan- or Aztec stone salt. Serve in a flute or wine glass.

Ingredients (serves 1)

70 ml honey-fed water kefir
· 50 ml Blue Clitoria tematea flower water · 20 ml Psilocybin (truffle) lemon-tek (1,5 gr truffle per serving) · 4 ml coconut syrup · 2 ml Lion's mane tincture (per serving) · Optional: a vitamin B3 (niacin) chaser

If you're growing your own kefir, feed it with some honey and dried fruit, top up with water and leave for a day or two at room temperature (in a pressure-safe bottle and skip the shaker when preparing if you want it fizzy). On the day, siphon off the watery part that you'll be working with.

To create the Psilocin lemon-tek, start by slicing and chopping your truffles – the more surface area, the better - and soak them in fresh lemon juice. Make sure they're covered by the liquid and leave it at least 20 minutes (to up to a day in a fridge). Longer is better.

Soak 3-5 dried Clitoria ternatea flowers in hot water, let it cool down, then strain. Prepare your glass with a pure honey (or agave) rim dipped in desiccated coconut. Besides looking great with the blue drink, its texture and sweetness will make the truffle residue (should you add it) more enjoyable.

Combine all the ingredients in a shaker. Shake and strain with a coarse strainer. Serve in a large chilled flute or wine glass – it's feminine, like the drink. Optional: put the truffle residue in the drink for complete dosing.

Tips & Tricks

Water kefir: Like kombucha, water kefir is a probiotic drink generated by a symbiotic colony of bacteria strains called a scoby. It's bursting with beneficial enzymes and acids and is excellent for hydration and maintaining the systems of the body. You can buy kefir from health food stores or maintain a colony yourself. Don't combine with MAOi (Monoamine oxidase inhibitors are a class of drugs that inhibit the activity of one or both monoamine oxidase enzymes).

For centuries, Blue Clitoria has been used as a memory enhancer, nootropic, anti-stress and antidepressant.

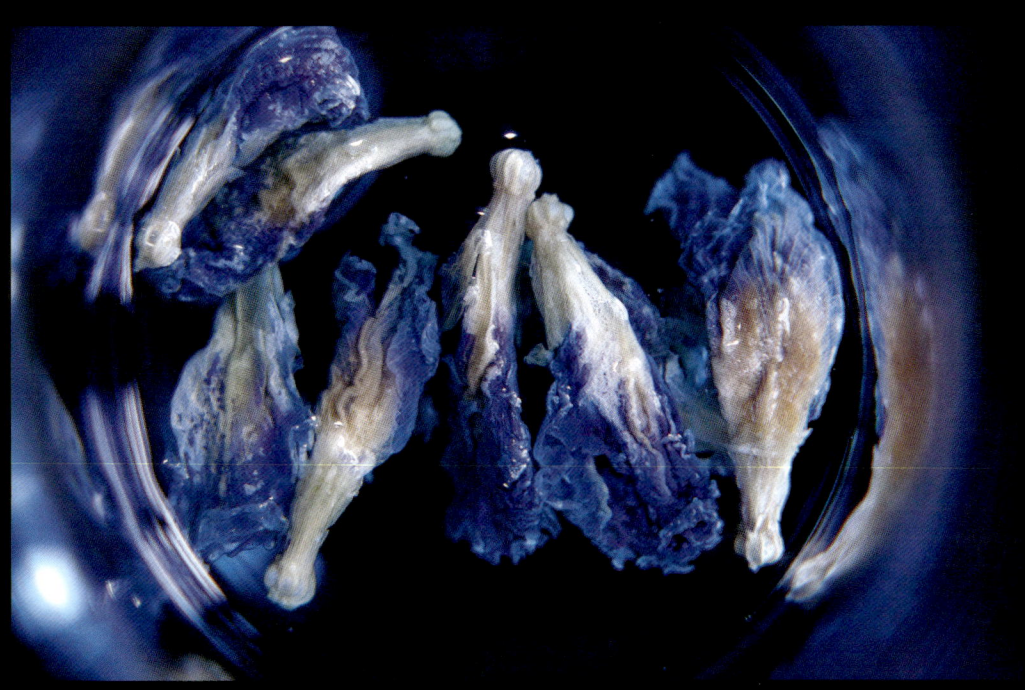

Mixologists & Recipes

Sgt. Pepper

Herb
LSA Seeds

High
Strong

Flavour
Tangy

Lucy in the Sky with Diamonds. We all know what it refers to. But did you realize that Sgt. Pepper is a reference to LSH, based on naturally occurring LSA in seeds? The recipe of LSH is an elusive thing: how to get from A to H, from sedative to euphoric. With mint, Peppermint. Serve in a coupette.

Ingredients (serves 1)

150 morning glory seeds · 6 Hawaiian Baby Woodrose seeds · 8 Ololiuqui seeds · 240 ml distilled, fractally imploded water · some lemon juice or ascorbic acid · 10 gr freshly muddled mint · 3 drops of peppermint tincture · 3 drops of aged rhum · 3 gr clavohuasca · 3 gr camomille · add cardamom, fennel, ginger, saffron to taste

Grind the seeds to a fine powder and put them in a tea bag. Correct the accidity of the cold, distilled, fractally imploded water to 4 pH (75ml) with lemon juice or ascobic acid. Infuse the grounded seeds under constant movement for about 40 minutes, then remove the seeds.

Add drops of peppermint tincture and rhum. Store in a light-blocking glass bottle in the fridge for a minimum of 8 hours, a day is better.

Make a 165 ml infusion of the clavohuasca and camomille. Add cardamom, fennel, ginger and/or saffron to taste.

Combine the different preparations in a shaker. Shake and strain with a coarse strainer. Serve in large chilled coupette or martini glass – Make sure it stays below 20°C. Garnish with a rose.

Tips & Tricks

Make sure it stays below 20°C, otherwise the 'LSH' will fall back to 'LSA'.

Effects
Expect effects in about 2 hours: euphoria without many visuals, but with enhanced hearing and sense of smell. Take good care of set and setting.

Cold water extraction
The magic of a euphoric LSH trip, without (much) body-load is a relative short cold-water extraction of the seeds, that are combined with a peppermint tincture and left

(contd.)

overnight in the fridge. Cold and dark is key. So long as your extraction does not go on for too long, the nauseating non-polars will stay inside the teabag. Put aluminum foil around the jar to shield it from light. It is super helpful to test some of your solution under a blacklight. The indole in the extraction glows bright whitish blue.

Seeds

You can opt to work with only one LSA containing botanical: 300 morning-glory seeds, 8 Hawaiian Baby Woodrose seeds, 20 Ololiuqui seeds for a full dose divided in three drinks. Make sure that you know and trust the source of your botanicals. Seeds from the garden store are doused in chemicals and unfit for consumption. It is, however, very possible and highly recommended to grow your own from garden-store bought seeds.

Grinding

Grinding these seeds is not quick and easy. Use a mortar and pestle or a coffee grinder.

Ayahuasca

Herb	High	Flavour
Chaliponga, Chacruna, Mimosa, Caapi, Rue, Cannabis	Strong	Sweet, Tangy, Bitter, Earthy

This book is about cocktails, and they usually taste nice. The challenge, to me, is to work with the taste profile of the various botanicals and give them an honourable place in a composition of tastes, colours, textures and experience. This recipe makes the botanicals both functional and palatable. When I first felt a calling for this medicine and tasted it, I felt an inspiration to one day make my own recipe. Well, there you have it.

Ingredients (serves 1)

25 gr Chaliponga · 100 gr Chacruna · 25 gr Mimosa · 8 gr Caapi · 5 gr Rue · 8 gr Clavohuasca · 4 gr Lapacho · 3 ml fresh ginger juice · 1 leaf of fresh mint · 2 gr of a fresh vanilla pod · 1 big black cardemom pod · ascorbic acid · 1 drop of cannabis tincture · fractally imploded or water from sacred sources · your choice of green-apple, banana, blood-orange and/or anis-syrup

For this version of ayahuasca various sources of DMT and MAO-i (see section - Safety: Plants Beat Drugs) are utilized. It is an intentionally complex recipe. It is important to be in a very good state of mind while preparing the brew, with no distractions. Take the phone off the hook. There are various bases/ recipes that are later combined. Bring about 3,5 liters of water to pH 5 with some acorbic acid.

Base 1
Crush, by whatever means available, but preferably by hand, Mimosa, Caapi and Rue. Put 50 ml water and the botanicals in a jar and regularly move/shake it for about an hour. Strain off the water and keep separate.

Base 2
Combine the botanicals from base 1 with about 1 liter of pH-corrected water. Crush, preferably by hand, the Chaliponga and Chacruna. Add the leaves and gently bring to a boil. Boil for 20 minutes. Strain off the water and put it in the different pot that will simmer at around 85'C to vape off most of the water. Repeat 3 times.

Boil down
Simmer the brew at around 85'C to vape off until about 600 ml is left. Filter the brew through various sifs and filters. Let is sit for 6 hours to a day so a sediment forms. Carefully siphon off the liquid. Reduce the brew by simmering until about 200 ml is left. Pour the brew in a bottle, combine it

(contd.)

(above)
Psychobria Viridus

(right)
Banisteriopsis Caapi
shredded bark from Peru

with the liquid from Base 1, cap it well and pasteurize it for about 15 minutes above 73°C. The liquid will become nicely transparent and stable.

In a pestle, crush the Clavohuasca and Lapacho, Black cardamom, the seeds of the vanilla pod the Camomille and the mint. Pour 50 ml of hot water over it and let it infuse and cool, then fine strain. Add the ginger juice.

Combine the transparent ayahuasca and the infusion, add a drop of cannabis ticture and bring it to taste with a syrup of choice. Shake and serve. Garnish with a Fugu-fin, if you are lucky to find one. Set your intention and let go.

Tips & Tricks

Ayahuasca is Sacred. Soma is the elixir of immortality. The quintessence of medicine is the combination of functions of different botanicals to disrupt fundamental axioms. Enjoy a flying carpet cocktail about 20 minutes before this ayahuasca recipe for added functionality. Watch your diet the days before and after consumption.

Effects

Expect effects in about an hour, sooner with a flying carpet as a primer. You may experience enhanced visuals, hearing, sense of smell, and profound teachings. Take good care of set and setting. Unlike alcohol or weed, these botanicals are, in my opinion, not 'recreational' or 'comfortable' and not to be toyed with. They are teachers who ask you to be sincere, pay attention and not be afraid. But that should not prevent you from enjoying the experience! Almost inevitably, the purging that comes with ayahuasca, is to be embraced, not scrubbed out of the experience. It will so profoundly alter your consciousness that the whole nausea thing is somewhat beside the point.

Tess Posthumus
Amsterdam, The Netherlands

Tess Posthumus is the epitome of modern bartending superstardom, with a cabinet full of national and international trophies, two books to her name (Cocktails with Tess and Masterclass: Cocktails) and her own range of bar utensils. When she's not running her two bars in Amsterdam, she travels the world as a freelance hospitality consultant.

While studying Media & Culture at the University of Amsterdam (a Master's in Sociology followed in 2014), Tess fell in love with the wonderful world of mixology.

Turning her side job into a career, she worked at the legendary speakeasy bar Door 74 in Amsterdam before taking the leap with fellow Door 74 barman Timo Janse to open their own place - Flying Dutchmen Cocktails. At this elegant, high ceilinged 17th-century merchant's house, Tess and her team focus on neo-classic cocktails and building up Dutch cocktail culture.
In August 2020, her second bar opened its doors, Dutch Courage on Amsterdam's Zeedijk, where the focus is on Dutch spirits and their heritage, Jenever in particular. An unrepentant history geek, Tess loves nothing more than delving into the stories behind the drinks and the spice trade pioneered by the Dutch East India Company (VOC).

"We were involved right from the beginning of booze, and the VOC spread our Jenever and liqueurs around the globe, even using them as currency."

She sees the use of home-grown exotic cocktail ingredients like cannabis and truffles as an extension of the Netherlands' trading and high-tech agricultural prowess, pointing out that the royal family once owned opium and cocaine factories.

"We've always been there, not always positively, but innovative and focussed - and we can be a bit cheeky if it makes money."

Tess is also an in-demand hospitality consultant (co-)owner of Perfect Serve Barshow Amsterdam, Difford's Guide Netherlands and Amsterdam Cocktail Week.

High Chai

Herb
Blue Lotus

High
Medium

Flavour
Spicy, Creamy, Sweet

Blue lotus was originally found on the banks of the Nile in Egypt. Nowadays, most blue lotus comes from Thailand and India: the land of the chai. While working as a consultant for an international tea brand, they taught me how to prepare a proper cup of chai and introduced me to all the variations and options this category includes. I noticed that while there are so many different ways of preparing a chai, they also had one major thing in common: all chai's had relaxing, soothing and calming effects. It might have been the therapeutic preparation method of creating a smooth rhythm while throwing the chai. It might also have been the milky element. Maybe the relaxing effects of hot milk are the actual reason Cleopatra loved her milk baths as she did? The milk used in this High Chai is flavoured with Indonesian inspired spices, which works beautifully with the aniseed flavour notes found in the blue lotus tea. The result is this High Chai, a perfect dessert-style cocktail or before bedtime drink. Especially if you take the hypnotic-sedative and aphrodisiac effects of the Blue Lotus into consideration.

Ingredients (serves 1)

100 ml spiced chai milk · 100 ml blue lotus tea · 100 ml Java black tea

Spiced Chai Milk
1000 ml milk · 300 ml condensed milk · 30 gr gulu djawa (Indonesian palm sugar) · zest of 1 orange · 2 cm fresh ginger · 6 cloves · 5 whole black peppercorns · 3 green cardamom pods · 2 whole cinnamon sticks · 1 whole star anise · 3 green cardamom pods · 2 whole cinnamon sticks · 1 whole star anise

Blue Lotus Tea
5 gr dried blue lotus · 100 ml water

Add the ingredients to two chai mugs and throw or "pull" the High Chai. Pour into a large tea mug or toddy glass. Garnish with some freshly grated nutmeg on top and a mini stroopwafeltje (Dutch cookie) on the side.

Spiced Chai Milk
Crush the cardamom pods and chop up the ginger and gulu djawa. Add the cloves, black peppercorns, cardamom, cinnamon and star anise to a pan and toast over medium heat. Once the spices start to release their fragrances, add the milk, ginger and orange zest. Add the condensed milk and gulu djawa while continuing to stir. You don't want the sugar and heavy condensed milk to stay at the bottom of the pan and burn. Keep stirring until both are dissolved. Fine strain or scoop out the spices and zests before use.

Blue Lotus Tea
Brew a strong tea from the dried blue lotus flowers and boiling hot water. Steep for 5-10 minutes

Tips & Tricks

If you "pull" the milk and tea mixture by throwing it from one canister into the other one, back and forth, you'll get a very nice foamy head on top of the chai. The throwing will mix the two liquids together, cools it down a bit and aerates it. Practise a bit beforehand with water (easier to clean off the floor than sweetened milk), or use a cappuccino milk foamer machine if you're too scared to try.

Make sure to make a strong brew of the Java black tea. Use 2,5 grams or one teabag per 200 ml boiling water, and steep for 4 minutes.

I used a Java black tea because its flavour profile works lovely with the spices used. Another reason I used this Indonesian tea is because it has enough backbone to add depth and balance out the overall drink.

Kratom is a tree, and the leaves are chewed or ground up in a powder. It increases your energy, focus and boosts your brain's performance. No wonder that this herbal cocktail turns you into a euphoric powerhouse. Inspired by one of the signature cocktails from my Dutch Courage Bar (the Grassy Lowlands cocktail), this green concoction uses the bitterness of the kratom tea as a backbone to balance out its refreshing kick. Veggies and cracked black pepper will get you started, followed by a juniper berry, sage and bay leaf herbal note, while the kratom completes the experience when it takes effect.

Ingredients (serves 1)

50 ml cold kratom tea (see recipe below) 50 ml green bell pepper juice · 30 ml lime juice · 30 ml juniper berry, sage & bay leaf syrup (see recipe below) · 1 dash black pepper tincture (see recipe below)

Juniper Berry, Sage & Bay Leaf Syrup
4 gr juniper berries · 4 gr dried sage 1 dried bay leaf · 500 gr sugar · 250 ml water

Cold Kratom Tea
2 gr kratom powder · 100 ml water

Black Pepper Tincture
100 ml 96% neutral grain alcohol · 10 gr whole black pepper

Shake all ingredients in a cocktail shaker filled with cubed ice. Fine strain over cubed ice into a rocks glass. Garnish with sage and freshly ground black pepper on top.

Juniper Berry, Sage & Bay Leaf Syrup
Add all ingredients to a pan over medium heat and stir occasionally. Dissolve sugar into water. Don't let it come to a boil. Fine strain, cool and store in the fridge in a clean glass bottle until use.

Cold Kratom Tea
Brew a strong tea from the kratom and boiling water. Give it a good stir and let it sit until cool. Store in the fridge while preparing the rest of the cocktail ingredients.

Black Pepper Tincture
Add black pepper and neutral grain alcohol to a clean glass bottle and leave to infuse for a minimum of 3 weeks. Shake the mixture whenever possible.

Strain after the infusion period and pour into a clean glass bottle until use.

(contd.)

Tips & Tricks

Substitute the 96% alcohol with a food-grade glycerine for a non-alcoholic black pepper tincture.

Can't find any 96% neutral grain alcohol? You can also use vodka. Because vodka has a lower ABV (Alcohol by Volume) percentage, you might need to up the amount of black pepper used or leave it to infuse for a bit longer.

Use freshly juiced green bell pepper and lime juice. The bitterness of the kratom tea needs the freshness of the juice to balance it out. When you leave it out for too long, the green bell pepper and lime juice will oxidise and both get an extra bitter and off flavour.

For a medium high, I suggest consuming 2 gr of kratom powder. But as 2 gr will enhance the bitterness of the cocktail, rather drink two cocktails instead of upping the dosage of kratom tea used. And you'll get some extra vitamins in the meantime. Everybody wins.

I've used a powdered Maeng Da kratom, which is a very powerful one from Thailand. If you're using a less potent version or a non-powdered kratom in plain leaves, you can up the dosage to 3-5 grams.

Kanna is originally from South Africa and was used by the Zulu and San tribes to help relax and recharge after a long day of hunting. It is sedative at low doses and euphoric at higher ones, ensuring that Kanna first gives you energy, followed by a smooth feeling of relaxation. With this in mind, I wanted to create a cocktail to honour the story of Kanna and South Africa.

The combination of South African style tea, red wine, blood orange, and spices work beautifully with Kanna's liquorice flavour. Enjoy this cocktail when you're looking to recharge and relax.

Ingredients (serves 1)

45 ml rooibos tea · 20 ml mulled red wine syrup (see recipe below) · 20 ml blood orange juice · 20 ml lemon juice · 15 milligram kanna extract

Mulled Red Wine Syrup

1 whole nutmeg (grated to taste) · 1 whole cinnamon stick · 3 cloves · 1500 gr sugar · 750 ml red wine (preferably a full bodied South African wine)

Shake all ingredients in a cocktail shaker filled with cubed ice. Fine strain into a pre-chilled coupe glass.

Garnish with a blood orange slice with 15 milligram Kanna extract powder dusted on top. Eat the slice while sipping on your cocktail and enjoy the ride.

Mulled Red Wine Syrup

Add the cloves, cinnamon and nutmeg (grated to taste) to a pan and toast over medium heat. Once the spices start to release their fragrances, add red wine and sugar. Stir to dissolve the sugar into the liquid. Don't let it come to a boil. Fine strain, cool and store in the fridge in a clean glass bottle until use.

Tips & Tricks

Make sure to make a strong brew of the rooibos tea. Use 2,5 grams or one teabag per 200 ml boiling water, and steep for 5 minutes. Because the Kanna extract is drunk and eaten, instead of snorted, it will take a bit longer for it to work. Patience is key.

Kanna extract is used in this cocktail. This powdered Kanna is on average ten times stronger than normal Kanna, explaining the low dosage of 30 milligrams for this cocktail.

Cowabunga

Herb	High	Flavour
Cannabis	Light	Tropical, Fruity

I am a bartender from the Netherlands, and although our ocean doesn't have a nice reef break, and 90% of the time, our weather is cold and wet, I do love to surf! With this Cowabunga cocktail, I'm trying to channel some of the positive vibrations a good surf session brings me, through the liquid inside your glass, into your body and mind. And what better way to do this than by using some of the age-old stereotypes surrounding the surfer's culture. This cannabis cocktail is a little liquid wink to the stereotypical stoner culture of surfers while including the tropical settings of my dreams and honouring the ocean with a small savoury note and seaweed garnish (seaweed; see what I did there?). And even though this cocktail asks you to do a bit of preparation beforehand, trust me, it truly is worth it. Proost, cowabunga, and keep riding that wave!

Ingredients (serves 1)

60 ml Seedlip Spice 94 non-alcoholic spirit · 30 ml passion fruit syrup & cannabis-coconut oil mixture* · 30 ml fresh lime juice

Passion Fruit Syrup
Pulp of 3 fresh passion fruit · 500 gr sugar · 250 ml water

Cannabis-Coconut Oil
300 ml unfiltered coconut oil (the ones that are still raw and smell like coconut) · 3 gr cannabis

Passion fruit Syrup & Cannabis-Coconut Oil
200 ml passion fruit syrup · 30 ml cannabis-coconut oil · 0,5 gr xanthan gum

Shake all ingredients in a cocktail shaker filled with cubed ice. Fine strain into a pre-chilled coupe glass. Garnish with a quarter of passion fruit and half a rim of sea salt & seaweed**

Passion Fruit Syrup
Add all ingredients to a pan over medium heat and stir occasionally. Dissolve sugar into water. Don't let it come to a boil. Fine strain, cool and store in the fridge in a clean glass bottle until use.

Cannabis-Coconut Oil
Chop up all the cannabis into small pieces. Slowly melt the coconut oil in a pan above medium heat. Add the chopped up cannabis and give it a good stir. Slowly heat the mixture until 180° Celsius. Set aside to cool down. While still solid: strain through a cheesecloth or coffee filter and store in a clean glass bottle until use. Use 3 ml per portion for a nice medium high (on average, depending on the THC and CBD levels of the cannabis you've used. I've calculated it with strong Dutch weed).

(contd.)

Passion fruit Syrup & Cannabis-Coconut Oil Mixture*. Mix all ingredients until you're left with a homogeneous solution.

Sea salt & Seaweed

Blend a mixture of 50% sea salt with 50% dried nori seaweed sheets until you have a fine powder. Store cool and dry until use.

Tips & Tricks

Make sure the sea salt & seaweed rim is only on the outside of the glass. I only use half a rim, so you can have some sips with sea salt & seaweed, and some sips without. Whatever you're in the mood for!

Mix the cannabis-coconut oil into your passion fruit syrup with some xanthan gum so the oil won't solidify when chilled (after shaking with ice). This way, the oil creates a beautiful and tasty creamy layer on top of the drink, instead of turning into solid parts if you don't use the xanthan gum to mix the two ingredients together beforehand.

Magic Floribbean Lemonade

Herb
Magic Truffles

High
Medium

Flavour
Sour, Spiced, Fresh

Magic truffles originate from Florida but are now exclusively grown in the Netherlands. As a proud Dutch bartender, who always longs for warmer climates, I wanted to add some of the exotic spices found in the Floribbean pantry in this far fetched riff on the (originally Dutch genever based) Collins cocktail. A nod to the truffles origins and the places my mind travels to after the truffles start their magic.

Ingredients (serves 1)

60 ml pineapple juice · 30 ml lemon tek* · 15 ml cinnamon & allspice syrup** · top up with ginger ale

Cinnamon & Allspice Syrup

3 whole cinnamon sticks ·
6 whole allspice berries ·
500 gr sugar · 250 ml water

Shake all ingredients in a cocktail shaker filled with cubed ice. Strain over cubed ice into a sling glass and top up with ginger ale. Garnish with a dried pineapple slice & physalis.

Cinnamon & Allspice Syrup

Add all ingredients to a pan over medium heat and stir occasionally. Dissolve sugar into water. Don't let it come to a boil. Fine strain, cool and store in the fridge in a clean glass bottle until use.

Tips & Tricks

Make sure to use fresh pineapple juice, as this also adds some sourness to the drink. If you don't have a slow juicer to press some yourself, and your only option is store-bought juice, add a bit extra lemon juice to the cocktail for balance. You want your lemonade to have a sour character

Ben Warren began his bartending career when he took a job in a generic Wetherspoon's pub (a nationwide chain in the UK) and found he loved working with drinks and spirits but especially loved the whole social aspect of hosting guests.

He ditched the Wetherspoon's, upgrading to a job at The Living Room, a more salubrious high-volume cocktail bar and restaurant in Angel Islington, London, with a training program and a 120-cocktail menu to sink his mixological teeth into.

He spent two summers working in Ibiza as a bartender. He later moved to Amsterdam and has never looked back.

Following positions as a bartender at several of Amsterdam's finest bars, including Door 74, Feijoa and Porem, he took on the role of Bulleit Bourbon Brand Ambassador at Diageo, doing bartender training and cocktail events.

In 2018 he brought all this previous hospitality experience together and founded Duke of Tokyo, a mock-up of the typically maze-like back streets of Tokyo, with eight karaoke booths based on the city's districts (Roppongi, Harajuku, Shinjuku, etc.).

He and his partners opened a second location of Duke in Utrecht, with more in the pipeline.

At the Dukes, he likes to include a Japanese element where possible in the drinks and keep the menu fun, light-hearted and tasty.

Early Morning Call

Herb
Kanna

High
Light

Flavour
Coffee, Earthy, Floral

Most of us are coffee fans. Some of us love drinking Espresso Martini's when we're out. It helps give us that morning surge or evening lift. Think of this drink as a sort of turbo-boosted healthy espresso. Adding the Kanna extract helps elevate mood and alertness whilst decreasing stress and tension. This can be a perfect early morning jump starter or evening pick me up!

Ingredients (serves 1)

40 ml Beetroot Juice · 50 ml Espresso · 30 ml Kanna & Cacao Syrup · 3 drops Rose Water · 1 pinch of rock salt

Kanna & Cacao Syrup
100 gr cacao · 500 gr sugar 500 gr water · 5 gr kanna

Combine all ingredients into a cocktail shaker and shake with ice. Pour into a cocktail glass, making sure you get a nice foamy top. Garnish with a little sprinkling of rose petals and powdered sugar if needed.

Kanna & Cacao Syrup
Firstly crush up the cacao beans before combining the crushed cacao, sugar and water together and bring to a simmer for around 30 mins. Take off the heat and allow it to rest for about 20 mins. Strain the syrup so it is clear of any bits before adding and stirring in the Kanna. Best

Eye of the Beholder

Herb	High	Flavour
Kratom	Light	Fresh, Tropical & Herbaceous

A refreshing take on a fizz style cocktail incorporating a carrot & tarragon syrup with the addition of Kratom to help give a subtle boost and keep you feeling alert going into the night. Combined with Aquafaba as a vegan replacement to egg white to help give the drink a light and fluffy texture. Shaken with a couple of slices of chilli (optional), and the top up with Ginger Beer helps give it a slightly spicy aftertaste. Serve in a tall glass.

Ingredients (serves 1)

80 ml Carrot & Tarragon & Kratom cordial · 20 ml Pineapple Juice (unsweetened) · 30 ml Lime · 15 ml Aqua Faba (liquid from chick peas) (optional - shake with 3 slice chilli) · 70 ml approx Ginger Beer · Garnish with Tarragon leaf and dehydrated pineapple

Combine 1000 ml water 20 gr kratom and let simmer for 15 mins. Add 600 gr sugar and add the 400 gr of carrot peels and cut pieces and 15 gr tarragon. Leave to simmer for another 15 mins and then let rest, stirring occasionally for 1 hour. After 30 mins add in the citric acid. Fine strain and cheesecloth to get rid of any small bits and bottle. Make sure to shake before using.

Blue Da Ba Dee Tea

Herb	High	Flavour
Truffles & Blue Lotus	Medium	Refreshing, Floral, Earthy

The oldest printed recipes for iced tea date back to the 1870s and were included in two of the earliest cookbooks, Buckeye Cookbook and Housekeeping in Old Virginia. As its popularity grew in the years following, there were many variations on the classic tea, sugar and lemon formula. During the prohibition era in the United States, it was not uncommon for people to spike their iced teas with alcohol which at the time was illegal. Fast forward many years, and this is likely where the Long Island Iced Tea originated from. Think of this as a spiked iced tea without the booze that will change colour over time to just play with your mind. Best served in a long sling-style glass.

Ingredients (serves 1)

30 ml shiso & peach cordial (recipe below) · 100 ml floral iced tea (recipe below) · 15 ml lemon · 50 ml soda · garnish - shiso leaf, candyfloss, butterfly · blue lotus & butterfly pea tea ice cubes

Shiso, Peach & Truffle Cordial
225 gr peach · 30 gr shiso · 400 gr sugar · 400 gr water · 8 gr tartaric 4 gr citric · 4 gr salt

Floral Iced Tea
1000ml boiling water · 2 gr lavender · 30 gr Chrysanthemum · 4 gr jasmine

Blue Lotus & Butterfly Pea Tea Ice Cubes
20 gr Blue Lotus
20 gr Butterfly Tea
500 ml hot water

Add all the ingredients together (see recipes below) into a sling glass, top with soda and for an electric final touch toss in the Blue Lotus & Butterfly Pea Tea ice cubes.

Shiso, Peach & Truffle Cordial
Peel and dice the peaches, add to the 400 gr sugar & water and let stew for 15 mins. Add the ripped up shiso leaves and let sit for another 15mins. Fine strain to get rid of the shiso and peaches and add the acids and salt. Adjust to personal taste if required.

Floral Iced Tea
Combine all ingredients into a container and add hot water (boiled water that has been left to cool for a few minutes is ideal). Let sit for 4 mins and then fine strain through a cheesecloth. Add the truffles and let rest for approximately 30 mins before straining again, remembering to keep the truffles that are leftover to dry and use as garnish or just have alongside the drink. Keep refrigerated in the bottle.

Blue Lotus & Butterfly Pea Tea Ice Cubes
Combine all ingredients into a container and add boiling water. Let sit for 5 mins and then strain. After the liquid has cooled, pour into ice cube moulds of your choice and freeze.

(contd.)

Tips & Tricks

Crush or cut the truffles as small as possible. The smaller you make the truffles, the better and quicker the psychedelic substances in the almond milk will be absorbed. You can also let them rest in a small amount of lemon juice to help them interact with the active ingredients and increase their solubility. Try to use fresh ingredients for the floral tea. It will taste a bit bitter, but it will balance out once you've added it to the cordial drink.

Magic Moon Shake

Herb	High	Flavour
Truffles & Mushrooms	Medium - Strong	Tropical, Rich, Creamy

We all know and love a good milkshake and have probably heard about the infamous mushroom milkshakes of Koh Phangan in Thailand. Well, this is a take on one of those, combining some easy techniques to create some unique flavours that can be adapted with other oleos or ice creams depending on preference. Add some homegrown mushrooms to the Almond milk and sprinkle the truffles/mushrooms on top for that extra kick.

Ingredients (serves 1)

150 ml Truffle infused Almond Milk · 10 ml Banana Oleo · 10 ml Mushroom Syrup · 1/2 banana · 1 scoop ice cream (Salted Caramel) · Garnish - Mint Sprig, Mushroom Candy, 100's & 1000's

Truffle Infused Almond Milk
20 gr truffle · 1 litre unsweetened almond milk · 10 gr dried homegrown mushrooms (optional)

Banana Oleo
50 gr caster sugar · 3 banana peels · 1 stick cinnamon · 3 cloves

Mushroom Syrup
50 gr dried Bolets & Cepes mushrooms · 500 gr sugar · 250 gr water

Put all the ingredients in a blender and mix until it's all broken up and there are no more chunks in it. Serve in footed high ball glass.

Truffle Infused Almond Milk
Take 20 gr of truffle and muddle/grind it up and add to 1 litre of unsweetened Almond milk. Bring to a simmer and then take off the heat. Let rest for 90 minutes and then fine strain through a cheesecloth. Transfer into a clean bottle and refrigerate. Make sure to give it a good shake before use.

(Dehydrate the leftover truffle pulp so it can be used as a sprinkle on top of the finished drink. You can always add 10 gr of dried homegrown mushrooms after taking the almond milk off the heat and let them sit in the truffle almond milk for 90 minutes for some extra kick. Make sure to use it within 2 days.)

Banana Oleo
Add 150 gr of caster sugar, 3 banana peels (approx. 180-200 gr), 1 stick of cinnamon and 3 cloves to a sealable plastic container and let sit for 24 hours, shaking occasionally. The sugar will extract a lot of flavour out of the peels, and after, you'll be left with a pretty intense delicious banana syrup. (Yield is approx. 125 ml - 150 ml)

Mushroom Syrup
Take 50 gr of dried Bolets & Cepes mushrooms and add to 500 gr of sugar and 250 gr of water. Let it simmer for 20 minutes * until all the sugar has dissolved, and then let

(contd.)

it sit for another 30 minutes, stirring occasionally. Fine strain cheesecloth to make sure there are no tiny bits left and bottle and refrigerate.

Tips & Tricks

Crush or cut the truffles as small as possible. The smaller you make the truffles, the better and the quicker the psychedelic substances in the almond milk will be absorbed. You can also let them rest in a small amount of lemon juice to help them interact with the active ingredients and increase their solubility.

Naushad Rahamat
Antwerp, Belgium

In 2012, native Amsterdammer Naushad Rahamat was well on track to his chosen career in hotel management, with three years learning the ropes in the city's prestigious 5-star Okura Hotel coming straight after his studies.

Then love - and a TV show - led to a dramatic change of mind. He decided to move to the home town of his Antwerp girlfriend, and he watched the final of the Diageo World Class Competition, the biggest cocktail making competition in the world.

"I'd enjoyed making cocktails at the Okura," he says, "but watching this final really demonstrated what was possible, the level of creativity that could go into the profession." From then on, cocktails became his passion.

Arriving in Antwerp in 2013, he immediately landed a position at Cocktails At Nine, the best bar in the city, if not the whole of Belgium, and rapidly worked his way up to head the bar team.

By 2017 he was competing in the competition that had inspired his career change, chosen as Best Bartender in Belgium to represent the country at the Diageo World Class final, where he came 12th from 55 entrants.

He subsequently made a move to the small screen as a presenter on the culinary TV show Njam!, for whom he covers the craft and history of cocktails for Dutch and Belgian viewers.

Today, besides training new talent at Cocktails at Nine, he's busy running Craftails, a pre-made cocktail company he established in 2020 and developing new flavours in his own laboratory.

With its famous art and fashion academies, the creative city of Antwerp, Naushad believes, is the city (outside of the Netherlands) most likely to adopt the High Cocktail concept.

"I've watched how popular mocktails have become, and adding 'high herbs' is a great way to generate a good vibe. They're a nice alternative to alcohol; I've enjoyed learning how they can be used in a similar controlled way – strong or weak, and these ingredients have a great future."

Try to Beat Thyme

Herb
THC

High
Medium

Flavour
Bitter, Sweet, Fresh

This bittersweet cocktail is a perfect balance between the earthy notes from the beetroot and a subtle hint of thyme. The grapefruit juice adds freshness to the drink and slightly enhances the bitterness from the tonic.

Ingredients (serves 1)

50 ml cranberry juice (good quality) · 20 ml beetroot syrup (see recipe below) · 70 ml tonic water · 3 sprigs of thyme · 5 ml THC syrup · 15 ml fresh grapefruit juice

Beetroot Syrup
1.5 kg red beetroot · 500 gr sugar · 500 ml water

Place all the ingredients in a shaker except for the tonic, give it a vigorous shake, pour into a tall glass full of ice, top off with the tonic water and garnish with thyme, and set it alight, creating a fragrant aroma while consuming your cocktail.

Beetroot Syrup
Peel and thinly slice the beetroot, put into a saucepan with the sugar and water. Place the pan on the stove and bring to a boil. When this is ready, set the pan to simmer and cook for thirty-five minutes. Then set aside to cool. Once cooled, strain it through a fine sieve and decant it into a bottle and place it in the fridge for later use.

Lady Kombucha

Herb
Truffles, Kratom

High
Strong

Flavour
Sweet, Sour, Tropical

A beautiful and elegant cocktail which is far more exciting than a glass of champagne. The rhubarb and coconut give it a complex taste that feels tropical and fresh. The kombucha brings the fizz and adds some depth to the drink. Serve in a champagne flute glass.

Ingredients (serves 1)

20 ml seedlip · 40 ml rhubarb & coconut cordial (see recipe below) · 20 ml kratombucha · 2 gr chopped truffles

Rhubarb & Coconut Cordial
1 bottle rhubarb juice (from Nahmen if possible) · 200 gr grated coconut · 15 gr citric acid · 250 ml fresh milk · 350 gr castor sugar · 10 gr grated coconut for garnish · 1 lemon

Using a cut lemon, rub an even strip around the flute. Starting from the base of a champagne flute to the rim and dust with the coconut.

Add the chopped truffle to the flute, place the coconut cordial and seeds in a shaker with two ice cubes and vigorously shake for five seconds. Strain this into the champagne flute and top off with the kratombucha.

Rhubarb & Coconut Cordial
Place all the ingredients into a saucepan except for the milk. Put the pan on the stove and bring to a boil. When ready, drop to a very light simmer and cook for thirty minutes. Strain the syrup through a fine sieve. Place the milk in a bowl adding the syrup to the milk to curdle. Place the bowl in the fridge, cover, and allow to sit for twenty-four hours. Take the syrup and strain it through a coffee filter or cheesecloth. The result should be a clear liquid. Set aside for later use.

Peach Leaf

Herb
Kratom

High
Light

Flavour
Sweet, Fresh

White peach juice combined with the fragrant bay leaf lifts you out of the mundane, transporting you onto a boat on the Amalfi coast. The Kombucha brings the sparkle making this a drink you can enjoy day and night before or after dinner. Just sit back, close your eyes and enjoy!

Ingredients (serves 1)

40 ml seedlip · 40 ml white peach & bay leaf cordial (see recipe below) · 20 ml kratombucha · 10 ml kratom tincture · 20 gr melted white chocolate

White Peach & Bayleaf Cordial
1 bottle white peach juice (Nahmen) · 10 gr citric acid · 10 gr tartaric acid · 400 gr castor sugar · 20 bay leaves (fresh if possible)

Take a coupe and paint the outside of the glass with the white chocolate to your desired design. Place the kratom tincture in the glass, add the rest of the ingredients except the kratombucha into a shaker with two ice cubes. Shake vigorously for five seconds, strain into the glass and top with the kratombucha.

White Peach & Bayleaf Cordial
Place all ingredients into a saucepan, place on the stove, bring to a boil; drop to a simmer, and cook for 35 minutes. Set aside and allow to cool. When cool, place in the fridge for twenty-four hours. Strain the syrup through a fine sieve and decant it into a bottle. Set aside in the refrigerator for later use.

East meets West

Herb
Kanna

High
Light

Flavour
Sweet, Sour, Refreshing

With this drink, it's all in the name. The cordial inspired by the Asian cuisine, combined with the typical German riesling grape, blends into an incredible refreshing highball with complexity.

Ingredients (serves 1)

40 ml seedlip · 30 ml coconut & kaffir lime cordial (see recipe below) · 5 ml Riesling grape juice (Nahmen) · 30 ml soda water · 1 gr kanna extract · 2 lime leaves

Coconut & Kaffir Lime Cordial

1 litre coconut water · 200 gr grated coconut · 12 lime leaves · 500 gr castor sugar ·

Place all the ingredients into a shaker except for the soda shake vigorously and strain into a glass full of ice cubes and top off with the soda garnish with lime leaves.

Coconut & Kaffir Lime Cordial

Place all the ingredients into a saucepan, place on the stove, bring to a boil; drop down to a simmer, and cook for one hour. When the syrup is ready, allow it to cool and strain through a fine sieve. Decant into a bottle and set aside in the fridge for later use.

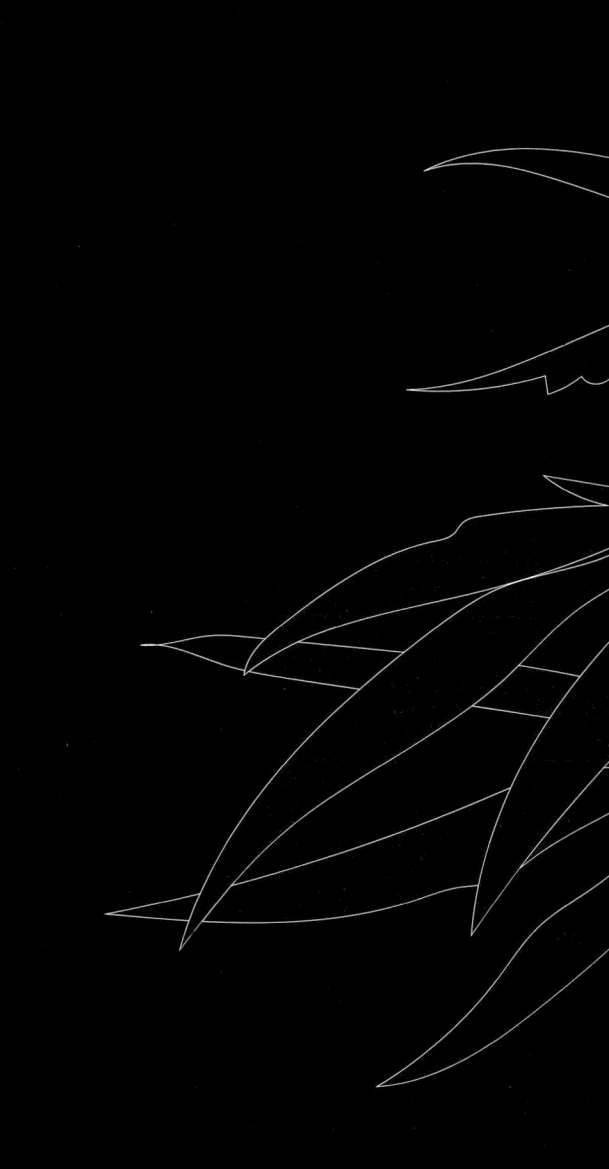

Plant Index

Ayahuasca — 122

Blue Lotus — 124

Blue Clitoria — 126

Cannabis — 128

Coca — 131

Guayusa — 133

Kanna — 134

Kratom — 137

The LSA Seeds — 139

Magic Mushrooms — 142

Magic Truffles — 144

Syrian Rue — 146

Ayahuasca

Banisteriopsis caapi, Psychotria viridis (plus various additives)
Active ingredients: harmaloids, DMT, 5-MeO-DMT, bufotenine and others

Ayahuasca is just one of various names used by many indigenous peoples of South America for a generic cocktail of two or more herbs that produce a variety of visionary experiences.

The brew generally consists of the non-psychedelic Caapi vine (there are at least 20 subspecies) and a source of (the powerful psychedelic) DMT, usually Chacruna (P. viridis), of which there are also many subspecies. Bear in mind that like all plants, they also contain a range of similar chemicals and others that can either boost or inhibit the 'main' desirable one that together acts as an entourage.

Taken on their own, neither the herbs nor the vines do anything spectacular. But a certain plant alchemy happens when they're boiled together for several hours in water, and the 'ayahuasca spirit' is born.

Its psychoactive action is generally explained in Western terms as (temporary, reversible) enzyme-inhibition by substances in the vine, slowing the DMT breakdown enough to manifest its visionary action. This easy-to-grasp biochemical equation: vine + leaf, or enzyme inhibitor + psychedelic, is a vast over-simplification of what is a complex and highly variable concoction embedded in a wide range of native cosmologies.

To complicate things, shamans brewing ayahuasca will often add a third herb, such as tobacco or datura, or more. These create a whole spectrum of ayahuasca's, plural. Coupled with the many different tribal names, wide geographical areas and range of uses, the oral transmission of what is often a secret recipe, and the importance of songs, rituals, incenses and diets attached to its ceremonial or healing use, have a vastly more complex story than science suggests.

To simplify it once more, it's like the vine is a microscope, and the DMT is a light. Together they can be used to 'see' into the essence of well, anything: another plant, an ill person, the future, spirits of the dead. Tribes even added petroleum when it first found its way into the Amazon so that they could perform an energetic analysis on it.

So don't get too hung up on a precise recipe if you choose to make it yourself. When asked where they got the recipe and how they (or their ancestors) managed to find just the right combination of the thousands of rainforest species around them, shamans universally reply that "the plants told them".

Blue Lotus

Nymphaea caerulea
Active ingredients: nuciferine and aporphine

This species of water lily is believed to originate in East Africa. Once common growing in the shallows of the Nile, today it is scarce in the wild. Easily propagated, it had spread to other locations even in ancient times, such as the Indian subcontinent and Thailand, where today it is commercially farmed.

The Blue Lotus is also known as the blue Egyptian lotus, blue (Egyptian) water lily and sacred blue lily of the Nile. It was prominently featured in ancient Egyptian art, especially in the tomb of Tutankhamun, whose mummified body was found garlanded with flowers when his tomb was opened.

Until the late 1990s, it had been regarded as purely symbolic (of the sun god Ra) by archaeologists; there is no proof in any papyri that the Egyptians knew it was psychoactive.

Evidence that they did comes from the fact that the lotus is often depicted in scenes with other powerful plants or in 'party' scenes of wine and debauchery. It was not until 1998 that Professor Andrew Sharrett demonstrated a consciousness-altering effect in his TV documentary Sacred Weeds. Participants in the programme exhibited a relaxed body with an active mind and were chatty with an elevated feeling of well-being.

The reported effects are quite subtle: a pleasant feeling of warmth around the head and upper body; a comfortable, dreamy feeling and an expanded state of consciousness, mildly sedative and euphoric.

BLUE LOTUS
Nymphaea caerulea

Blue Clitoria

Clitoria ternatea
Active ingredients: various triterpenoids, anthocyanins and steroids.

Clitoria is a genus of plants native to tropical and subtropical Asia, and by introduction now found in Africa, the Americas and Australia. And yes, they were named for their flowers' resemblance to female human genitals, hence the name 'Clitoria' from 'Clitoris'.

Rumpf, a German-born botanist working for the Dutch East India Company, first described and named Clitoria in 1678, and it still exists in many local languages. While there have been controversies as to the tactfulness of the name, Clitoria remains. For the easily embarrassed, it is also known as Blue Butterfly Pea, Asian Pigeon Wings, Blue Bell Vine, Cordofan Pea and Darwin pea.

The most widely used species is C. ternatea. When its petals are added to water, they impart a beautiful blue colour, which is part of the reason we use it here. In Thailand and Vietnam, it is made into a caffeine-free tea mixed with honey and lemon, the acidity of which turns the blue to a pinky-purple.

Clitoria merits inclusion on our psychotropic herbs list; used for centuries as a memory enhancer, nootropic*, stress-buster and antidepressant. According to Ayurvedic medicinal practices, its root aids tranquillity and is mildly sedative.

Substance that improves cognitive function, such as memory, creativity or motivation, in healthy individuals.

BLUE CLITORIA
Clitoria ternatea

Cannabis

Cannabis sativa
Active ingredients: Tetrahydrocannabinol (THC), Cannabinol (CBD)

Cannabis is the one herb many have experienced in one form or another. But no matter how well you think you know this herb, there are some essential factors to bear in mind when consuming it as a drink.

We love working with cannabis; even though High Cuisine is about utilizing a wide variety of mind-expanding herbs, cannabis still forms the base layer of our multi-course dinners and recipes. And now we've even incorporated it into our drinks.

Cannabis famously whets the appetite, and for this exact reason, a cannabis cocktail makes an ideal aperitif. It also makes a great party starter, thanks to another welcome effect of cannabis: its enhancement of conviviality. Being (lightly) stoned increases chattiness, loosens the laugh reflexes and generally lubricates any social event.

What creates that cannabis effect? Cannabinoids do. And they are produced in tiny resinous glands concentrated in the plant's female flowers. After the drying and curing are complete (usually done by its grower), moderate heat (usually via smoking or cooking) is needed to 'activate' the cannabinoids.

The heat initiates decarboxylation, whereby the non-psychoactive THC-acid in a raw herb transforms into THC, the molecule that generates the high. Since our cannabis cocktails do not use heat in their preparation, you will need to decarb your weed in advance (see Techniques).

CANNABIS
Cannabis sativa

You also need to separate the cannabinoids from the vegetable matter of the bud. The complication here is that cannabinoids are not soluble in water. Anyone who has ever tried to clean a water bong knows, cannabinoids are very resistant to mixing with water.

Soaking it in alcohol creates a tincture of cannabis, which does mix fine with water and is suitable for use in drinks. In its heyday, the late 19th-early 20th century, cannabis tinctures were popularly consumed as medicine before cannabis was banned worldwide.

If you don't want to use an alcohol-based tincture, you can use vegetable glycerin, apple cider vinegar or distilled white vinegar instead. Glycerin gives the mixture a sweet flavour, and vinegar adds a note of acidity, which works well with many cocktails. In cannabis cuisine, extracting cannabinoids can be done using fats such as butter & olive oil, or dairy.

Cannabis has tremendous genetic variability across its two main species, C. sativa and C. indica, creating a wide range of effects and aromas among varieties. Broadly, Sativas create a more 'energetic', mental high, making them best suited to social events. Indicas generate a more 'stoned' bodily high and are more suitable to solitary enjoyment. Most modern varieties are a blend of the two.

There are important issues to be aware of when serving cannabis drinks to a group, such as tolerance developed by regular consumers and the differences in effect between smoked and orally consumed cannabis (see Dosage chapter).

Observe these words of caution - especially if you're an experienced consumer and perhaps susceptible to over-confidence. Cannabis makes a marvellous, adaptable cocktail ingredient with a range of pleasant effects.

Coca

Erythroxylum coca and E. novogranatense
Active ingredient: cocaine, various alkaloids

There are two species of cultivated coca, each with two varieties. Which variety is grown where is determined by altitude and rainfall, each being adapted to highland or lowland, dry or wet conditions. In practice, they are all very similar in appearance and may have a common ancestor as yet undiscovered.

While not a psychedelic, we felt it was interesting to include as one of our herbs because it has a rich past and great future. Around the end of the 19th century it was an ingredient in a number of popular drinks that delivered a mild, caffeine-like buzz.

Traditionally cultivated for its power, coca combats fatigue and altitude sickness; rich in calcium, potassium, phosphorus, vitamins (B1, B2, C, and E) and so high in protein that it is used as a flour in regional cuisine. Coca is rightly considered a superfood and even an essential herb for living and working high in the Andes.

Coca has also been a vital part of the religious cosmology of the Andean peoples of Peru, Bolivia, Ecuador, Colombia, northern Argentina, and Chile from the pre-Inca period through the present. Coca leaves are a crucial offering to the mountains, the sun, or the earth (Pachamama). It also serves as a powerful symbol of indigenous cultural and religious identity amongst a diversity of tribes throughout South America.

Spirit Plants

COCA
Erythroxylum coca

Traditionally, coca leaves are chewed as a quid (held between the gums and cheek) or toasted, ground to a fine powder and mixed with an alkali (ash, baking soda or roasted, ground shells). When chewed, coca acts as a mild stimulant and suppresses hunger, thirst, pain, and fatigue.

....

Guayusa

Ilex guayusa
Active ingredients: caffeine, L-theanine, theobromine

Guayusa is a small tree (related to holly) that grows in the rainforest of northern Brazil and Ecuador. It has recently been growing in popularity in the West as an alternative to energy drinks and coffee.

The leaves make an excellent stimulant tea with a mild flavour and a pleasant aroma reminiscent of maté tea. But the main attraction of Guayusa leaves is less their taste than their eye-popping caffeine levels - up to 7%, the highest known concentration of caffeine in any plant.

If this sounds a bit harsh, fear not. In contrast to coffee, the caffeine in the tea is released more slowly, giving a more lasting, uniform effect. Guayusa also contains L-theanine, an amino acid that imparts a feeling of pleasant tranquillity, as well as theobromine (the 'happy' chemical also found in chocolate).

The combination creates a light, smooth stimulation, gentle performance enhancement and an overall vitalizing effect that makes it a natural aphrodisiac.

Thanks to various natural ingredients, Guayusa's effect ranges from stimulating to relaxing. It also has a much more agreeable pH than coffee, making it more digestible - even in large volumes - which is how the native Ecuadorian Jivaro tribe take "Nightwatchman," as they call it.

The Jivaro tribes folk gather around a large communal pot, chugging the tea while telling each other stories as a daily event and morning ritual that helps to reinforce kinship and community.

....

Kanna

Sceletium tortuosum
Active ingredients: mesembrine, mesembrenone, mesembrenol

Kanna is the name given to the fermented roots and leaves of the South African bush Sceletium tortuosum once they have been dried and ground to powder.

The result is a traditional vision-inducing euphoriant that can be taken in various ways for a spectrum of effects. It is increasingly used in the West to improve mood and reduce anxiety.

Kanna has been used by pastoralists and hunter-gatherers for relaxation, promoting social bonding for well over 1,000 years, and warriors returning from battle, who took it to help dispel what we now call PTSD, typical after violent conflict.

Traditionally, dried Sceletium was chewed, and the saliva swallowed. It was also added to smoking mixtures with other psychoactive plants, like cannabis and possibly wild dagga (Leonotus leonurus) to generate the more 'hallucinogenic' effects attributed to Sceletium.

Kanna potentiates alcohol and cannabis, which means you need substantially less of these substances to get the same effect. It also combines well with other smokable herbs like damiana and blue lotus flowers - mixtures that can also be enjoyed in drinks.

The first known written account of the plant's use was in 1662 by the Dutch explorer/trader Jan van Riebeeck. He started to barter with local tribes for it after finding out about its effects on stressed individuals and called it kougoed, or 'stuff for chewing'.

KANNA

Sceletium tortuosum

Kanna can be purchased as a powder, used as a snuff, smoked or made into a tea. Snuffed or smoked, the effects come on rapidly (a couple of minutes) and last for an hour or two, creating a mild, MDMA-like euphoria (with less of the effusive outpouring of emotion!) that fades to an almost narcotic state of relaxation.

As a drink, Kanna is less effective, and more of the product is needed to reach the same effect as when it is smoked or sniffed. It should be drunk on an empty stomach to work, and the results tend to be less euphoric and more sedative, analgesic and narcotic. It might take longer before effects appear (sometimes up to 1.5 hours), and in general, the effects last quite long: up to 4 -5 hours after ingestion.

Kanna contains several alkaloids responsible for its spectrum of effects, mesembrine, mesembrenone and mesembrenol being the most significant. Kanna powder can be enhanced with a 10x extract of these alkaloids, and since this reduces the amount of plant material, we exclusively work with extracts in our drinks.

Several Kanna extracts commercially available differ in their general effects depending on which alkaloid is prominent. For example, mesembrine is a serotonin-uptake inhibitor (SRI) and is the main ingredient of the UC and UC2 extract. It is responsible for the sedative effects of Kanna.

Being a Serotonin Re-uptake Inhibitor, Kanna should not be combined with pharmaceutical (S)SRI's or Monoamine Oxidase Inhibitors (MAOI's).

....

Kratom

Mitragyna speciosa
Active ingredients: 7-hydroxymitragynine, Mitragynine

Kratom is a tree with a rich and no doubt fascinating history. Unfortunately, very little of it was written down.

The kratom tree grows in Southeast Asia, where its leaves have been used as an energising and mildly psychoactive tea for thousands of years. A relative newcomer to the range of consciousness-altering herbs in the West, kratom is a subtle and intriguing plant with substantial medical and therapeutic potential and a nice recreational buzz that many find useful for focus or relaxation.

In its native Asia, it has been chewed or brewed into a tea as herbal medicine to treat pain, boost energy, alleviate anxiety and symptoms of depression, and promote wellness and happiness.

Amsterdam botanist Pieter Korthals wrote the first study of the plant while in service with the Dutch East India Company in Malaysia in the 1830s, after noting a lot of locals chewing it. He named it Mitragyna speciosa because he thought its flowers resembled a mitre or bishop's hat.

It's only since the early 2000s that kratom has made its way with any regularity into the US and European online and offline smart shops supplied from Thailand and Bali. The kratom from Bali is generally more of a mellow experience than the comparatively energetic Thai kratom. Both are sold dried as loose-leaf tea, raw powder, or fortified with leaf extract.

Spirit Plants

KRATOM
Mitragyna speciosa

Like all herbal highs, the experience of kratom can vary from individual to individual and from occasion to occasion. There are also differences in batches of the herb and potency of different brands, plus its effects differ depending on whether the dose taken was low or high.

Like coffee, kratom is a mildly bitter pick-me-up taken at any time of the day. Rather than giving a caffeinated short-term energy boost followed by a crash, it delivers a more centred, calming experience.

At higher doses, it becomes progressively more relaxing, sedative and pain-relieving. The effects are felt both mentally and bodily and include a sense of inner warmth and happiness, pleasant thoughts, relaxed breathing and reduced mental chatter. Though not itself an opiate, it is for these opiate-like effects that it has become increasingly popular.

The overall experience is very relaxed, whether in social interactions or by oneself - some report an increased ability to focus and a calm but intense mental stimulation.

Although more than 25 alkaloids have been isolated from kratom leaves, the natural history of its use, clinical pharmacology and toxicology are poorly understood. Only a handful of scientific papers have been written about its effects and the centuries-long history of use.

Mitragynine was believed to be the primary alkaloid responsible for kratom's effects, it being the most abundant. In 2002, 7-hydroxy mitragynine was discovered to be the most significant substance. Despite being present in much smaller amounts, this minor alkaloid was found to be even more potent in its pain-relieving action than morphine.

....

The LSA Seeds

Morning Glory (Ipomoea violacea) &
Hawaiian Baby Woodrose (Argyreia nervosa)
Active ingredients: d-Lysergic acid amide (LSA),
Lysergic acid hydroxyethylamide (LSH)

Most people are familiar with the famous synthetic psychedelic Lysergic Acid Diethylamide (LSD), even if only by name. Less well known is that "Acid" is just one member of the Lysergamine family of molecules. Several cousins exist naturally in plant seeds and have their own psychedelic effects. For example, d-Lysergic Acid Amide (LSA), also known as ergine, is found in the seeds of specific Morning Glory varieties and the Hawaiian Baby Woodrose (HBW) plant.

MORNING GLORY
Ipomoea violacea

Each species has variants growing in different (tropical) parts of the world. Both are climbing vines bearing colourful flowers that produce seeds containing LSA and trace amounts of LSH (Lysergic Acid Hydroxyethylamide) and four of five similar ergoline alkaloids.

The seeds are commonly sold by (online) smart shops and consumed for their trippy effects. (They can also be found in regular garden centres, but these are treated with chemicals to prevent consumption, so stick to smart shops).

LSA's effects are similar to LSD, except more sedating, nowhere near as intense and producing an inner experience rather than the funky visuals. Some people familiar with LSD and mushrooms report that the seeds produce a 'deeper' sensation.

As a bonus, although LSA seeds are much milder in action and shorter in duration (6-8 hours) than LSD, unlike acid, they're legal to buy and possess (though not to consume). As a result they are growing in popularity as sources for psychedelic microdosing.

Both morning glory and HBW seeds have been used for millennia by shamans and indigenous communities from Mexico to Africa to Nepal to achieve altered, visionary states for divination, diagnosis, and performing energetic healing.

They became popular among American hippies in the 60s, who mixed them with other herbs to create Utopia Bliss Balls or made a peppermint tea that converted the LSA to LSH for a different effect. Known as Sergeant Pepper's Tea, we've recreated the recipe and made it into a more complex cocktail.

Magic Mushrooms

Psilocybe cubensis, P. semilanceata, and others
Active ingredients: Psilocybin and Psilocin

There are around 200 species out of the 10,000-or-so fungi that have been identified as having psychedelic effects. More are being discovered all the time, especially since we (science, medicine, public) started taking this magical quality seriously - which we are.

The majority of them are in the Psilocybe genus, from the Greek words psilos (bare) and kub (head).

Commonly known as shrooms, mushies, cubes, baldies (kaalkopjes, Dutch word) and fool's mushroom (various countries) – none of them matches the grandeur and reverence of the Incas' teonanáctl (Flesh of the Gods), the ancient Greeks' ambrosia (Food of the Gods) or the soma of the Sanskrit Vedas.

Whatever you want to call them, amateur fans and scientists agree: the psychedelic mushroom is a thing of magic and mystery.

The primary active ingredients of all Psilocybe mushrooms are psilocybin and psilocin (and to a lesser extent, baeocystin, norbaeocystin, and at least 30 other complex organic molecules found in trace amounts).

How these substances work is still relatively unknown, though big money is being poured into figuring it out (and patenting it). Psilocybin and psilocin are part of the tryptamine family. They bear a close resemblance to the neurotransmitter serotonin, and the primary effect seems to involve its inhibition.

MAGIC MUSHROOMS
Psilocybe cubensis

Once only accessible from the wild to intrepid foragers, magic mushrooms have been farmed commercially since the 1990s. Although this was banned in the 2000s, various legal, easy-to-use kits (just add water, wait, and harvest) became available.

Today's most commonly available mushrooms are P. cubensis, and P. semilanceata (a.k.a. Liberty Caps), which cannot be farmed, only picked wild.

....

Magic Truffles

Psilocybe cubensis (sclerotia)
Active ingredients: psilocybin, psilocin

Like their non-psychedelic namesakes, truffles are the underground parts or sclerotia of various fungi species, the best known and first to be marketed being Psilocybe tampanensis (Philosopher's Stones).

They were first grown commercially in the Netherlands in the mid-1990s. However, they were sold more as a novelty during what in retrospect was a Golden Age of psychedelic fungi, when a dozen varieties of fresh magic mushroom were available from the smartshops of Amsterdam.

Being scientifically 'not a mushroom', when the Netherlands made the sale, possession and consumption of hallucinogenic mushrooms a crime (2008), truffles remained exempt and off the list of controlled substances in the Opium Act.

While they're a little weaker than magic mushrooms, they tend to grow with more uniformity of ingredients, which makes their dosage more reliable and predictable.

Great news for the Dutch farmers who grow them and the veritable industry of therapists, ceremony leaders and microdosing advocates who've emerged to cater to (inter)national demand for legal 'conscious tripping'.

Today, many growers supply a range of truffle varieties (Mexicana, Atlantis, Pajaritos, Hollandia and Dragon), all derived from Psilocybe cubensis and with slight, subjective differences. Various distributors will also send them abroad in discrete packaging.

Of all our herbs, truffles (and mushrooms) deliver the most reliable and broadest range of psycho-activity.

Taste-wise, while better than shrooms, they're still pretty funky, kind of nutty and tangy. But since their active ingredients are water-soluble, they blend easily in any cocktail.

Spirit Plants

Syrian Rue

Peganum harmala
Active ingredients: harmala alkaloids

If there's a more tragically overlooked high-inducing herb than Syrian rue, we'd damn well like to hear about it!

Not only does this subtle but powerful herb have an amazing back story, but there is a list of positive health effects as long as your arm as well as remarkable qualities as a high cocktail ingredient. In addition, it's cheap, legal and basically contains exactly the same active substances as the vision-inducing ayahuasca vine (Banisteriopsis caapi).

Syrian Rue is one of the most frequently used plants in folk medicine worldwide. It is also becoming increasingly well known among the global psychedelic community for its effects when used alone, but more often for its ability to magnify the effects of other plants and fungi when taken together.

In our High Cuisine dinners, we have used a Syrian rue dish to enhance the effects of a subsequent psilocybin-rich recipe with excellent results. And the fact that its active ingredients are readily soluble in water earned it a place on our cocktails list too.

A low-lying shrub that produces white flowers and round seed capsules, Syrian Rue is believed to have originated in and around the mountainous regions of Iran Still, today it grows in many semi-arid areas of the world from Africa through the Middle East to India and as an invasive species in South America, Mexico, and Southern USA.

SYRIAN RUE
Peganum harmala

While various parts, including it fruits, root, and bark, have been used in folk medicine for ages, the bitter little black seeds sold in smart shops (and regular middle-eastern spice shops) interest us.

These are rich sources of water-soluble beta-carboline alkaloids responsible for most of their pharmacological and therapeutic effects. The most prominent of these are the harmala alkaloids harmine, harmaline and tetrahydroharmaline.

The alkaloid content of Syrian Rue has been shown to be psychoactive. In various in vitro and in vivo studies, it's indicated a wide range of effects on both the central and peripheral nervous system, including analgesia, mild hallucination, excitation, and anti-depressant effects.

These effects are due to the beta-carbolines temporarily inhibiting the monoamine oxidase enzyme (MAO) responsible for the breaking down and re-uptake of monoamines like serotonin and norepinephrine that are responsible for the experience of consciousness.

Harmalas can be taken on their own in many different ways to facilitate mildly psychedelic, introspective, and dream-like states of mind. At high doses they can induce visionary experiences (including the sensation of floating or flying, and enhanced telepathic powers), but also nausea.

Some people report that the harmalas produce strong sensations of embracing the present moment, a feeling of observing every moment unfold by itself.

While not a new or revelatory experience, it is a state of mind that can be used, for example, in meditation and for being more 'present' in nature. Leonardo da Vinci and Michelangelo claimed that rue's metaphysical powers improved their eyesight and creative inner vision.

WARNING: DO NOT COMBINE SYRIAN RUE WITH MAOI MEDICINE OR TYRAMINE-CONTAINING FOODS.

Mesmerising trails of harmine fluoresce under UV light, descending from Syrian Rue seeds in a glass of Flying Carpet (see recipe section)

Just a Dash

Temperance, Tonics and Tinctures

Two popes, the Czar and Czarina of Russia, US President Ulysses S. Grant, writers Emile Zola, Alexandre Dumas, Jules Verne, Emile Zola and Henrik Ibsen, inventor Thomas Edison, actress Sarah Bernhardt, the sculptor of the Statue of Liberty and 8,000 doctors worldwide - all gave glowing testimonials to the focussed energy of Vin Mariani, the first recreational cocaine product brought to market.

In 1863, on reading a paper on the effects of the coca leaf and seeing an economic opportunity, Corsican chemist Angelo Mariani created a "tonic" coca wine. Its recipe yielded a drink of 10% alcohol and 8.5% cocaine extract by volume (note: that's from the raw leaf, not a heap of white powder!).

But it wasn't the alcohol or the cocaine percentages which made Vin Mariani so potent, but rather the chemical combination of the two.

If cocaine is consumed on its own, it yields two principal metabolites: ecgonine methyl ester and benzoylecgonine. Neither has any discernible psychoactive effect. However, when cocaine is co-administered with alcohol, it generates a potent psychoactive metabolite, Cocaethylene. It is formed in the liver by the replacement of the methyl ester of cocaine by the ethyl ester, according to Cocaine.org, which explains: "Cocaethylene is a very rewarding agent in its own right, blocking the dopamine transporter and inducing euphoria. Hence coca wine drinkers are effectively consuming three reinforcing drugs rather than one."

Mariani's advertisements extolled the curative virtues of the product: "renewing, invigorating, nourishing, strengthening, refreshing" - much the same claims made by most patent medicines of the day. However, what made Vin Mariani really stand out was the celebrity media blitz, almost certainly the first marketing campaign of its kind.

He introduced his coca wine in the mid-1860s. By the mid-1880s, Mariani was the largest importer of coca leaves in Europe, and his Vin the most avidly endorsed tonic on both sides of the Atlantic.

Testimonials from eminent personages were so numerous that Mariani published them in handsome leather-bound volumes, replete with portraits and biographical sketches of the endorsers. These included the Prince of Wales, the kings of Norway and Sweden, and the commanding general of the British Army. Pope Leo XIII drank it for years, calling Mariani a "benefactor of humanity", and presented him with a gold medal.

Among the 8,000 doctors who swore to the virtues of Vin Mariani, the first surgeon to use cocaine for spinal anaesthesia was Dr J. Leonard Corning of

New York. He testified that: 'Of all the tonic preparations ever introduced to the notice of the profession, this is undoubtedly the most potent for good in the treatment of exhaustive and irritative conditions of the central nervous system.'

The success of Mariani's wine inspired many imitators. The most famous being Pemberton's French Wine Coca, which survived various American prohibition laws, the 1906 Pure Food and Drug Act, and growing public anxiety over the addictive qualities of cocaine to become Coca-Cola.

Vin Mariani was not as fortunate, and for all its celebrity endorsements, was put out of business. So popes and kings would need to find their pick-me-ups elsewhere.

The Soda Bandwagon

Colonel John Pemberton had been wounded in the American Civil War and became addicted to morphine. He also had a medical degree and vowed to find a substitute for the problematic drug. In 1885 at his drugstore in Columbus, Georgia, he registered Pemberton's French Wine Coca nerve tonic, possibly inspired by the global success of Vin Mariani, but additionally included kola nut.

The following year local alcohol prohibition laws were passed, and Pemberton responded by developing a non-alcoholic version of his wine sold as a patent medicine and marketed as "Coca-Cola: The temperance drink". Pemberton claimed it as a cure for morphine addiction and indigestion, nerve disorders, headaches, and impotence.

Its two key ingredients were cocaine derived from the coca leaf and caffeine from kola nut (also spelled "cola nut" at the time, hence the name Coca-Cola).

It was sold as a syrup to drugstores, whose soda fountains were popular at the time due to the belief that carbonated water was good for the health. For the first several years of its existence, Coca-Cola was only available as a fountain drink; it was not until 1894 that it was first sold in bottles.
It once contained an estimated nine milligrams of cocaine per glass (for comparison, a typical dose or "line" of cocaine is 50–75 mg.), but in 1903, the coke was removed. From then on, instead of using fresh leaves, Coca-Cola started using "spent" leaves – the leftovers of the cocaine-extraction process as a coca leaf extract, from the one manufacturing plant authorised by the US government to import and process coca leaves.

Kola nuts act as a (bitter) flavouring and are the original source of caffeine in Coca-Cola, containing about 2.0 to 3.5% caffeine. Having just removed the cocaine without complaint, the company became embroiled in legal battles with the government over the caffeine levels in its drink in 1911. After several trials and appeals, the company volunteered in 1916 to halve caffeine levels and pay the government's costs to avoid further litigation.

Hokey-Cokey Kola Syrup

Coca-Cola was originally sold as a syrup to apothecaries, diluting it with soda water as needed. While they took out the cocaine in 1903, the company still uses coca leaf syrup in its modern formula, but the zing has already been chemically stripped out.

Since we have access to a small supply of coca leaf from our friendly neighbourhood shaman, as well as kola nut, we thought: how about recreating an energising tonic?

We found a recipe for kola syrup that sounded tasty and we tweaked it, doubling the kola nut (for added caffeine), then added a modest amount of coca leaf. We had leaf powder but coca tea is readily (if technically, illegally) available at outlets.

The recipe also gave us an excuse to shop for spices at the marvellous Amsterdam apothecary, Jacob Hooy (est. 1743), with its wooden barrels and drawers full of herbs and powdered roots (including sarsaparilla).

The result is a delicious and energising soft drink, and a syrup that can be used in regular cocktails (note that mixed with alcohol, the coca becomes more powerful).

Ingredients
300 gr granulated sugar • 100 gr dark or light brown sugar • 480 ml water • Zest of: 2 oranges, 2 limes and 1 lemon • 1/4 tsp. ground cinnamon • 1/4 tsp. freshly grated nutmeg • 1 whole star anise • 2 tsp. ground kola nut • 3/4 tsp. lavender flowers • 1 tsp. sarsaparilla root, powdered • 10 gr dried galangal or 15 gr fresh ginger • 1 tsp. citric acid • 1/4 vanilla bean • 20 gr coca leaf powder or 40 gr of leaf tea

Method
Combine all ingredients in a metal saucepan and bring to boil; reduce heat and simmer for 15 minutes. Remove from heat, cover and allow to stand for 12 hours/overnight. Strain syrup through muslin, squeezing all the syrup from the mixture. Discard the solids, bottle and label the syrup (20 oz /600ml), which will keep for a month in the fridge. Dilute to taste; makes approx. 20 servings when topped with soda water over ice in a tall glass. Garnish with a lime wedge.

The sugar content comes out at approximately 20 grams per serving. This is half what a typical 12 oz. (350 ml) commercial cola can contains (38 grams or about 12 teaspoons!), usually in the form of high-fructose corn syrup. Feel free to reduce the amount you use for your syrup, but keep the same amount as the other ingredients.

Mushroom Tincture

If you're planning a social event or want the convenience of a concentrated psychedelic elixir for your personal use, a double tincture of water and alcohol is a simple solution (no pun intended).

A tincture allows many doses to be stored more accessibly than dried fungi and is easily added to cocktails as-is.

There are two main psychoactive alkaloids in magic mushrooms and truffles: psilocybin, which is water-soluble, and psilocin, which is too but to a lesser extent.

Neither compound breaks down under moderate heat (which is why mushroom tea works fine, albeit with a slight loss of activity versus eating the whole fungus). The compounds can also be extracted by cold water, given more time.

But there are many other substances in magic mushrooms: a whole "entourage" of them that work synergistically to create the mushroom's effects, including various terpenoids, phenoloids, beta-glucans, polysaccharides and other alkaloids in trace amounts.

Some of these are not so soluble in water but are in alcohol (as is psilocin). Our mushroom tincture will use both water and alcohol to get the fullest extraction of as many substances as possible.

The slow extraction involves leaving the mushrooms to soak in high-proof vodka for 2-6 weeks before straining the mushrooms, reserving the alcohol, then adding water to the mushroom residue. Distilled water is best, or boil tap water first to remove chlorine.

1. Weigh your mushrooms or truffles and grind them into powder (use a blender if they're fresh and use the alcohol to rinse them all out) to create the maximum surface area for extraction.

From the weight, you can calculate how many doses this represents. This will stay the same however much liquid you choose to use in the tincture.

2. Place in a glass container (large jar or Kilner-type is ideal) and pour in 1oz (= 30 ml) of high-proof vodka (or Everclear, though vodka is fine) for every 5 gr (dry) or 30 gr (fresh) of mushrooms.

3. Leave for 2-6 weeks before straining the mushrooms off (ideally, squeeze through muslin) and reserving the alcohol extraction.

4. Add 5-6 oz (150-180 ml) water for every 1oz of alcohol used in the previous step to a pan. Bring to boil for a minute, add mushrooms, then remove from heat and allow to cool.

5. Strain off mushrooms again and combine the alcohol and water extractions for your final tincture. It will be around the strength of beer (4-5%) if 100-proof vodka is used or wine (10-12%) if Everclear is used.

You can speed things up by doing both extraction steps together and using the same volumes of liquid as before. Put the ground shrooms and alcohol in a glass jar; boil the water and add to the jar. Allow to cool; an insulated coffee mug will keep the temperature up longer, giving a complete extraction.

If you plan to consume the same day (or if the cocktail recipe requires it), you can add an ounce of lemon juice to turbo-charge the brew with a so-called lemon tek. It will speed up the onset of effects, which may be a little more intense and generate a smoother trip.

Acidified water is a poor storage medium, and psilocin rapidly oxidises. If you want to store the tincture for a while, skip the lemon juice. You can freeze the strained extraction into ice cubes (and melt it into the lemon juice if and when desired).

Or pour into a Pyrex dish and set in the oven at about 200°F / 95°C until it's a small enough volume to fit in one easy-dose small bottle. Let's say you started with 10 dried grams and have 50ml of tincture; you can then add a 5ml squirt to your cocktail for a mild dose.

Psilocin and -cybin are pretty stable when kept out of the light, so the tincture should stay potent for weeks, if not months, in a dark bottle or fridge.

One final advantage of a tincture is that having tried it once, it's easy to replicate or adjust further doses (with a graded pipette) because you're using the same composition.

Lemon Tek

Lemon tekking is the practice of soaking truffles or shrooms in lemon juice (or other acidic liquid) before you consume them. It results in a faster onset (ten to fifteen minutes) and a more intense experience. (So not recommended for novices!)

How does it work?
Shrooms produce both psilocybin and psilocin. Psilocin is absorbed directly by the body to produce psychedelic effects. However, psilocybin must first be converted into psilocin before it can be absorbed. The conversion process, known as dephosphorylation, begins upon entering the stomach.

This is one reason why psilocybin mushrooms take about an hour before their effects begin when eaten whole.

The theory is that lemon juice (which has a pH of around 2.0) is acidic enough to convert psilocybin, the same way the stomach does (with a pH between 1.5 - 3.5 in humans), making the shrooms completely bioavailable upon ingestion.

Lemon tek cuts down on the onset time since your body doesn't need to spend time making that conversion. When a dried shroom is digested, your body simultaneously absorbs the available psilocin and works on converting psilocybin. Instead of absorbing the entire dose at once, there is a natural staggering that takes place.

Many people also believe that lemon tekking increases the potency of the shrooms, making the trip shorter but more intense.

Procedure:
Grind your mushrooms or truffles into a fine powder and place it in a glass. Fill the glass with just enough lemon juice to cover the powder Leave for 20 minutes, and stir every 5 minutes. Since the mixture is not very stable, consume it within 24 hours, or freeze it for use in the (near) future. Its potency will deteriorate over time. Pass the liquid through a coffee filter. Combine with other cocktail ingredients as directed by the recipe.

Water: The Key Ingredient

We've been encouraged for decades now to 'stay hydrated' by drinking water, but very little has been said about the qualities of water that we should be hydrating ourselves with. Is some water better than others? What properties should we measure to make such a decision? Despite the never-ending boom in bottled water brands and flavoured drinks and the ever-increasing 21st-century obsession with purity, authenticity, health & wellness, the quality of the water we consume remains largely undiscussed.

Since a large part of our products - and indeed the base of our biology - is water, its quality matters. Looking into what "quality" meant, we discovered the many ways it can be optimised. Not only does water need sufficient biologically essential minerals and purity, but its energetic state might also have an impact on the taste and even effect of the herbs in our drinks.

The properties of water are so remarkable that few mainstream scientists even want to study it for fear of coming up with findings that might relegate them to the fringes of academia, which is where we looked when started researching this overlooked ingredient in all cocktails. Maverick researchers like Dan Winter, Dr Masaru Imoto, and Austrian natural scientist Viktor Schauberger (1885-1958), whose long-neglected observations on the true nature of water have started to trickle back into contemporary attention.

Industrial Water is Dead

Schauberger noted 100 years ago that water was way more than just some static resource or a mere commodity to be piped, flushed or sprayed as needed. Beyond obvious characteristics of healthy water such as its purity, acidity and other chemical properties, there are energetic aspects of vital importance too. The bad news was that the very structure of modern water distribution, its industrial processing and delivery, creates energetically 'dead' water.

According to Schauberger, water is akin to blood in the human body - the most important life-giving and energy-empowering substance on the planet. Yet, with incorrect handling, it becomes 'diseased', affecting human, animal and vegetable life alike, causing physical decay and, in the case of people, their moral, mental and spiritual deterioration as well.

Schauberger sought to develop devices that, by the power of shape, form and motion alone, could mimic nature's processes. He believed that our technology moves everything the wrong way – exploding, heating, pressuring. His inventions used nature's quiet cooling, inward-spiralling suction motions instead, and the result was rejuvenating instead of destroying. He studied the phenomena of the fluidic vortices in streams and rivers, from which he developed "implosion technology" -

(right) Air bubble in water

the opposite of explosive technology. He didn't consider this an invention in the conventional sense, but "the renaissance of ancient knowledge lost over time."

According to Schauberger's philosophy, derived from his practical observations and discoveries, there are properties water must have to be deemed beneficial to health. It must be free of pollutants and have an alkaline pH to neutralise excess body tissue acidity from diets, stress and environmental pollution.

Water should be micro-clustered. Water does not exist as single molecules in isolation but as groups of molecules weakly bonded together. Typically, most tap water has clusters of upwards of 12 molecules, thanks to the very structure of modern water distribution: industrially processed and delivered through concrete, plastic and metal pipes. This water is not particularly beneficial for hydration of the body cells and lacks vital energy - in Schauberger's estimation, it's dead.

Water Whirled

He outlined several other chemical and magnetic attributes of healthy water to do with its oxidation/reduction potential and ionic composition. The bottom line is that you can rejuvenate unhealthy water into life-giving water by subjecting it to a whirling motion - and better still, vortexing it, based on the principles of nature, thereby restoring its life-energetic properties.

The device directs the water in a spinning vortex through a magnetic field (based on the Golden Mean and the Planck Constant, also referred to as Schauberger's Dream).

Wetter and better? Unlike regular tap water, this vortexed water is energetically 'alive'; it feels "wetter" and hydrates the body much more efficiently. Plants watered with it are reputed to grow 15-40% bigger, and according to Schauberger, consuming good health-promoting water can have a dramatic impact on health, with possible benefits to both lifespan and quality of life:

Better body hydration ensures water drunk has maximum beneficial effect (and by extension, better absorption of the goodies in our herbs). It boosts immunity by eliminating toxic metabolic wastes and reducing the impact of stress and environmental pollution. Consuming revitalised water also improves brain function (especially in children), improving focus and attention span. It can reduce the need for pharmaceutical medications and increase energy due to better body functioning. In the long term, there is a significant reduction in degenerative diseases.

Various devices are available that perform this rejuvenation, and our bartender Joost used one to create his cocktails. Together with the Bulldog, we created a new range of herbally-enriched sodas using this rejuvenating device.

Attention was shone on the weirdness of water by the 2005 New York Times bestseller The Messages in Water by Japanese scientist Dr Masaru Emoto. He used high-speed photography to discover that crystals formed in frozen water reveal differences according to the water's health and concentrated thoughts toward them. Water from clear springs and regular water exposed to loving words showed complex, colourful snowflake patterns. In contrast, polluted water, or water exposed to negative thoughts, formed incomplete, asymmetrical patterns with dull colours.

The idea that our thoughts, words and feelings can influence water molecules and positively impact the earth and our health was polarising It was enthusiastically received by people who had always assumed this to be the case and rejected by those for whom such an admission would be devastating to their economic, scientific and even spiritual worldview.

No wonder scientists are terrified of investigating the stuff, although a few are starting to defy conventional academic boundaries. Nonetheless, in the years since Dr Emoto's book, something of a 'New Science of Water' has arisen that continues to reach mind-boggling conclusions. They support ancient pagan and modern indigenous peoples' beliefs: water is a living force with intelligence and worthy of respect, if not outright reverence.

Towards a ceremonial relationship

Artist and author of The Secret Intelligence of Water (2021), Veda Austin, creates amazing artwork from and with frozen water, what she calls "Hydroglyphs", to reveal the language of water. She concludes water is "fluid awareness", an energetic force in everything.

Here is perhaps the relevance of these speculations to cocktails - we must move into a "ceremonial relationship" with it as we begin to contemplate the implications of living in a world that responds to our thoughts and emotions through water.

In summary, there are strangely compelling arguments that lead us to entertain the possibility that water is a psychedelic ingredient in its own right, given that psychedelic means 'mind-manifesting' - and that is what water does: manifest mind.

So maybe we should be paying attention not just to the quality of the water in our cocktail but to the thoughts and feelings we have while making and drinking it - because the cocktail might be listening and responding!

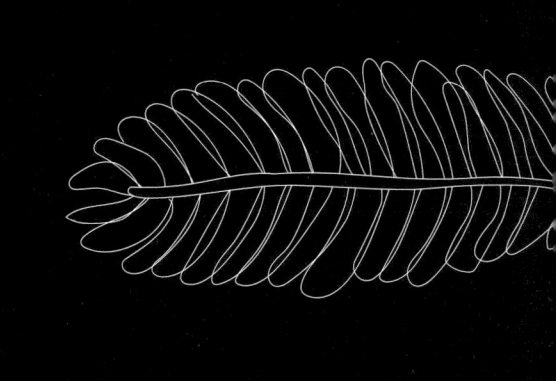

Too Much of a Good Thing

Dosage

Put to one side for a moment all thoughts of 'milligrams-of-X-per-kilo-bodyweight' when we talk about 'dosage'. While we have researched and tested our herbs, the real dosage advice can only come via self-experimentation.

Ultimately, you don't 'take' or 'do' herbs; it's about initiating a relationship with the plant or fungus, a new way of thinking about what we put inside us and what it does.

Plants are complex, multi-drug factories that pump out 100s or even 1000s of chemicals used for growth, defence, attracting pollinators and communicating with other creatures and their environment. Levels of these chemicals vary throughout the day; by the moon phase they were planted and harvested. Were they farmed or gathered in the wild, attacked by predators, or how long they were stored at each stage of their supply chain all have an impact? Fresh herbs are more potent than dried; active ingredients degrade over time and from exposure to light.

Once we step away from the comfort of pharmaceutical lab conditions, we're talking about a level of complexity and interaction that is beyond computation, making hard rules and amounts impossible, which is why 'about a gram' or 'half a teaspoon is about as accurate as we can be. However, that is not to say we can't suggest guidelines based on suppliers' advice, the experience of others shared online, and our own tasting sessions.

Whatever your motivation, an attitude of respect for these herbs is essential. Not only will this guide you in your decision making regarding dosage, but you will get more from the experience. Not just from the 'heavy hitters' like cannabis and truffles, with definite and noticeable effects, but especially from the more subtle herbs such as damiana or blue lotus. While some people rave about them, others feel little, if anything at first.

A certain tuning-in is needed to the plant's essence or effects; it may be that you need to 'meet the herb halfway' if that makes sense. A herb's effectiveness has as much to do with your mindset as it does with whatever the plant might bring to the table, chemically speaking. Don't expect them to do the heavy lifting for you.

Mushrooms/truffles - there are more than 200 species of fungi with psychedelic effects. The most commonly used are P. cubensis and P. semilanceata, the former tending to be weaker gram-for-gram. Our recipes used varieties of kit-grown Cubensis and commercially farmed truffles. There is a spectrum of effects depending on dose and aims; see the separate pages on psilocybin and LSA Seed dosage for details.

Entourage effects in cannabis and mushrooms combine in complex synergistic and agonistic results, even when consumed as a single herb.

These principles are best illustrated by cannabis, the high which comes primarily from THC content. But there are dozens of other cannabinoids also present in cannabis, and these modulate the THC experience. THC can produce an edgy, uncomfortable high. However, if consumed with a small amount of Cannabidiol (CBD), this edgy high immediately mellows to a more pleasurable experience.

The high is modulated by traces of cannabinoids, including another family of chemicals - the terpenes (responsible for cannabis's smell and taste). All these substances vary from strain to strain, age, and the weed's conditions, harvested and prepared.

In short, don't sweat the dosages of herbs too much as they vary from batch to batch, thanks to mood & atmosphere, tolerance and other x-factors, from event to event.

Magic Mushroom Dosing

Magic mushroom dosages are usually measured in dry grams since most people acquire them dried. Fresh ones are 90% water, so approximately 10 fresh grams equals 1.0 dry.

Magic truffles tend to be used fresh as that's how they are sold, in vacuum-packed, 15-gram portions. Since they have lower levels of psilocybin than mushrooms, a pack delivers one mild-to-moderate dose, equivalent to 10 grams of shrooms.

These are some figures that reflect online consensus regarding magic mushroom dosages. Of course, the "right" dosage depends on your tolerance and the kind of effects you want. To use the suggested doses below for your cocktails, figure out the strength of effect you want to arrive at, and divide that weight by the number of cocktails you want to drink to achieve that.

These weights apply to typical strength P. cubensis, the predominant species cultivated from kits and raised by underground growers. Bear in mind that dried fungi will lose potency with age. Weight-for-weight, the most popular species picked wild in Europe and North America (P. semilanceata, aka Liberty Caps,) are a little stronger than cubensis. So if you're using these, maybe drop the weights by 10%.

You can find detailed psilocybin/psilocin concentrations in mg.-per-gram of these and other less-frequently encountered psychedelic fungi online. These guidelines are enough to get you started safely and effectively.

Microdose (0.1 – 0.7 grams, dried)
This involves taking 10-20% of a moderate dose, which is imperceptible. But it still offers some of the mental benefits of psilocybin with minimal psychoactive effects.

"Social" dose (0.8 – 1 gram, dried)
Stronger than microdosing, but still only gives you very mild effects. You'll experience an enhanced mood and greater mental focus but won't experience hallucinations or a distorted sense of time or space. Our working dose for a single cocktail.

Moderate dose (1 – 2 grams, dried)
This is where you'll start to experience mild hallucinations as well as strong psychedelic effects. Still manageable but not overwhelming. Outbursts of hilarity not uncommon.

Psychedelic dose (2 - 3.5 grams, dried)

You may experience intense hallucinations and a warped sense of reality. This can be overwhelming for beginners; it's best to only experiment with this dose when you're in a safe environment.

Strong dose (3.5 - 5 grams, dried)

Going higher than 3.5 grams is unnecessary for most users and should be avoided unless your name is Terrence McKenna (who was an advocate of 5 dried grams - taken in darkness - as a cosmic, potentially enlightening but occasionally terrifying experience).

LSA seed dosage guidelines

The psychedelic effects of LSA (d-Lysergic Acid Amide), found in the seeds of Morning Glory and Hawaiian Baby Woodrose (HBW), occur less consistently than the better-known psychedelics like LSD or psilocybin mushrooms/truffles. Some seed packs aren't active; depending very much on the age, it has a limited shelf-life. Even when they 'work', the precise effects vary, probably depending on the various alkaloids' relative concentrations. But in general, the high is primarily bodily and cognitive, with minor if any visual effects.

Only use seeds from a smart shop; those sold in garden centres are treated with chemicals. Whichever LSA seed you choose, because its use is oral, onset is affected by the last food ingested (try not to eat at least 4-6 hours before consuming LSA).

If you're using HBW seeds, remove any remaining husk (scrape away or use a lighter to burn it off), and cut or grind the seeds into small bits with a knife, scissors or pulverise in a coffee grinder.

Hawaiian Baby Woodrose Seeds

	Seeds
Threshold	1 - 3
Light	3 - 6
Common	5 - 8
Strong	7 - 12
Heavy	12 +

Put the cut up seeds in a cup and pour half a cup of hot but not boiling water on them. Distilled water is better than tap water, but if you must use the latter, boiling it will remove any chlorine, which can diminish the effect of the seeds. Leave the mixture for at least 1½ hours for the water to cool down to room temperature. The alkaloids dissolve in the water during the cooling process. Strain the seeds through a coffee filter and discard.

The most common active Morning glory variety is Heavenly blue, which is also the most robust variety (others include Pearly gates, Flying saucers, Wedding bells, Blue star, and Summer skies).

Although Heavenly blue is the strongest variety, it is widely available and used here as a reference. Grind the seeds and make a water extraction as for Hawaiian Baby Woodrose Seeds, above, and use according to the cocktail recipe.

Morning Glory Seeds	Seeds	Grams
Light	50 - 100	1.5 - 3
Common	100 - 250	3 - 6
Strong	250 - 400	6 - 10
Heavy	400+	10+

Too Much of a Good Thing

Mood and Atmosphere

Psychedelics are not tools that do the same thing each time you consume them. It matters how and where they're used. The context we create for a psychedelic experience matters. The preparation we do, the intention we set, the kind of environment we choose – all these are factors in whatever we hope to achieve from a psychedelic experience.

Which is a roundabout way of saying that the first question to ask yourself regarding dosage is: Why are you taking this herb or fungus now? Just for fun, as a temporary respite from the world? For personal growth and exploration? For your psychological health or spiritual journeying? For connecting with nature? As a lubricant for socialising or as a solitary experience?

All are valid; we're not telling anyone why they should consume our herb-spiked concoctions, simply offering them tasty alternatives to how they might ingest them. It's also okay to have more than one motivation, to use the various herbs and fungi for different ends on different occasions.

We bring forth a fundamental concept in psychedelic practice: the importance of set and setting. It refers to the profound dependence of psychedelic effects on psychological, social, and cultural factors. In cocktail bar terms, we'd talk about ambience and mood; what's the place like in terms of music, background chatter, lighting and decor? How welcoming is it?

As an extension to the elements known as Set (your interior frame of mind, such as mood and motivation) and Setting (preparation, exterior aspects such as venue, music), some psychedelic trippers like to use rituals. Whether a mind-focussing blessing or incantation, clearing the space with smudged sage (or incense), lighting candles or placing ingredients on a home alter.

The very act of making any cocktail is inherently a ritualistic activity; why not play with this a little?

Some things to consider

These are a few issues and things to think about based on our many dinners and cocktail tasting sessions. Summarised as: planning is essential, know-thyself, particularly thine limits! As best you can, take into account that these will vary from individual to individual.

More practically, what time do you have available? Is the dose likely to be incapacitating? What do you plan to do during and after the experience? Bear in mind that cannabis and psilocybin effects can last up to 6 hours before you're back at your baseline.

Closer to the event, consider: when do you plan to eat? An empty stomach is generally recommended, but we've found having some food inside you can also reduce nausea. If you have our first book - Bites - you could also serve psychoactive hors d'oevres with your cocktails!

Creating good vibes

- Put together your favourite playlist of music. What non-psychoactive refreshments do you need to get in advance? Herb tea is great, and bear in mind that mixing alcohol and any powerful herb should only be attempted by those with mastery of both!

- If you're getting together with friends, how will you get together (and get safely home again)? Do you want to serve just one icebreaking cocktail at the beginning of the evening or drink 2, 3 or more? Think about the dose and effect you want to reach and work backwards, dividing that dose by the number of drinks you'll consume.

- Turn off your phone(s)! Psychedelics benefit from having a 'be here, now' mentality. You don't want the intrusion of a random call from the non-tripping world outside.

- How well acquainted with these effects are you (and any guests)? Keep in mind that drinking a substance takes longer to take effect than smoking it but less time than eating it as an edible.

Factor in Tolerance

Do remember to factor in any tolerance you might have built up. Stoners (regular consumers of cannabis) take note - your mild buzz may flatten your non-stoner friends. Mushrooms/Truffles need a week to clear from your system; retake them before that, and you need more for the same effect. Ditto for microdosing: if you do this 2-3 times a week, you'll need more than someone who has not recently been microdosing.

Will you drink 2-3 of the same cocktail and herb, or will you serve a combination of different cocktails with synergizing effects?

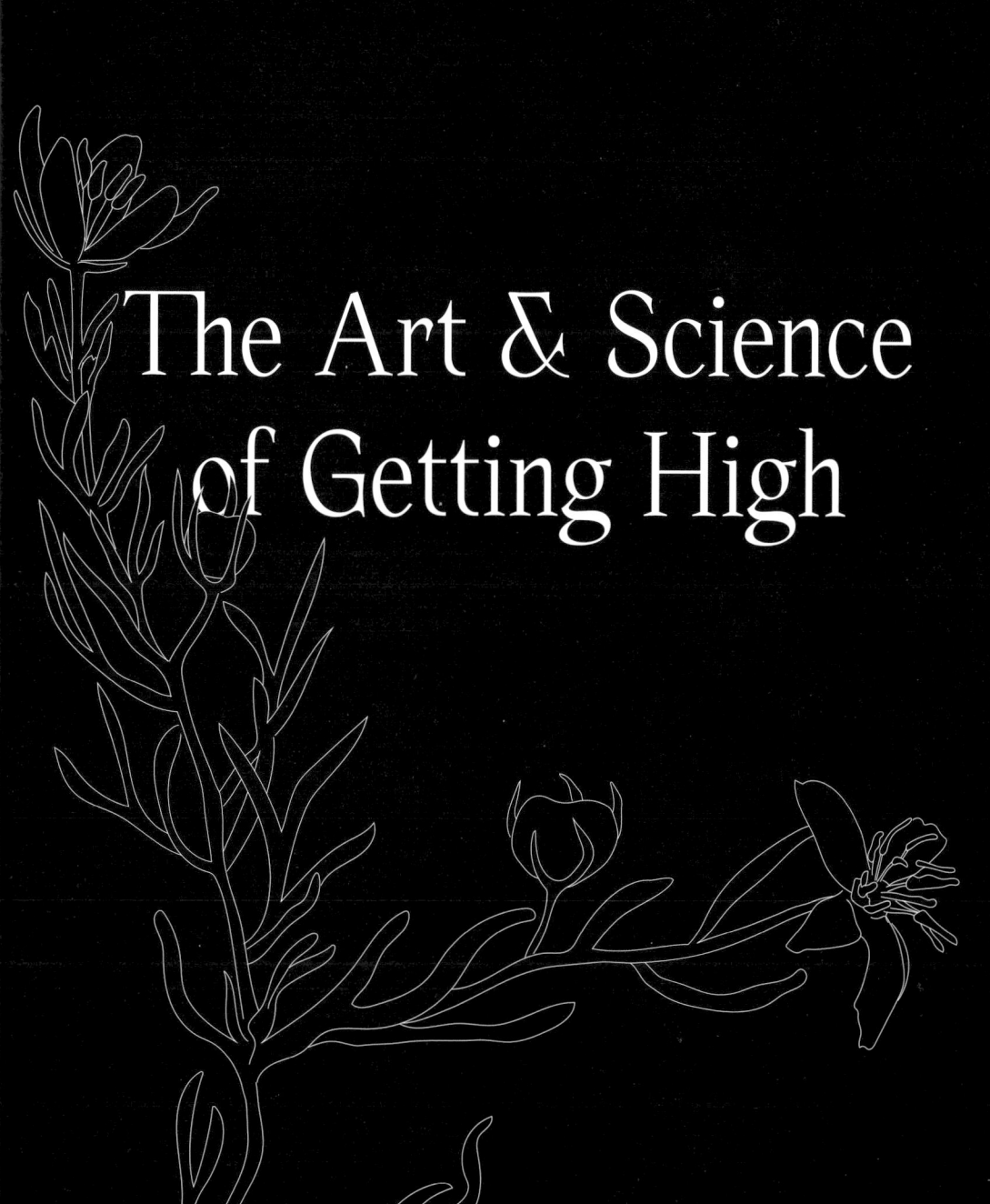

The Art & Science of Getting High

The Entourage Effects

Cocktails, as any bartender can tell you, are all about the blend and balance of ingredients. Even tiny traces - a glass rimmed with citrus peel, a couple of drops of bitters - can dramatically redefine the drinker's sensory experience.

As naturally occurring organisms, every cannabis plant, herb, and mushroom produce its own cocktail of chemical compounds — cannabinoids, terpenes, psilocybin derivatives, etc. Both chemical cocktails in cannabis and psilocybin mushrooms are said to work as an "entourage" in which the multiple active ingredients synergistically produce the effect experienced by the user. Their precise concentrations and balance strongly influence the experienced effects and are why different strains and varieties have a spectrum of potential effects.

If this were not complicated enough for you, various entourages could combine for further synergies and modulated effects - in other words, we can mix herbs and fungi in single drinks and combinations of drinks. The sheer complexity of hundreds of compounds merging with hundreds of other compounds, and so on, illustrates why hard-and-fast rules to dosage are less useful than a more experiential approach. And why we have a section on cocktail combinations.

The cannabis high

The cannabis plant contains at least 113 different cannabinoids, including THC and CBD. Tetrahydrocannabinol (THC) is the one mainly responsible for the plant's psychoactive properties. Cannabidiol (CBD) has been known to dampen some of the effects of THC, making it less intense. Higher CBD or lower THC levels will result in a less psychoactive and sedative high, for instance. Cannabis' sedative effects promote relaxation, often accompanied by heightened sensory perception and a warped sense of time.

The cannabis industry has only recently begun to appreciate how many lesser-known active ingredients (e.g., CBD, CBC, CBG, THCv) in cannabis can be more potent than THC and affect the overall high even in tiny amounts. In addition, so-called terpenes, compounds that had been regarded as solely responsible for the plant's odour and taste, were also found to chip in with phsysiological and psychological effects of their own.

As a result of this complexity, the high cannabis produces can be both euphoric and sedating at the same time. The intensity of effects will depend largely on the cannabinoid ratio found in the plant being consumed.

(left) Microscopic close-up image of the trichomes on a Jack Herer flower.
(photo by Hawoodrose)

The mushroom/truffle high

Magic mushrooms and truffles induce a euphoric and hallucinogenic high, primarily thanks to psilocybin and psilocin. Psilocybin is almost universally described as "the" (sole) active ingredient in magic mushrooms. Yet psilocybin is not the active ingredient. Instead, it is a prodrug (precursor) of psilocin, which provides the psychedelic effects.

When consumed, psilocybin is quickly converted to psilocin, and it is this that acts on serotonin receptors in the brain, partially activating several of them. Psilocin also indirectly increases the concentration of dopamine in the basal ganglia of the brain, producing the strong euphoric sensations experienced when ingesting magic mushrooms.

Shrooms and truffles also contain a cocktail of active molecules, including at least eight different psilocybin derivatives: terpenoids, phenoloids, beta-glucans and polysaccharides, and most recently discovered, a class of compounds known as ß-carbolines. These are most commonly known as components of the ayahuasca brew that inhibit the body's enzymes and makes it possible for the psychedelic compound DMT (dimethyltryptamine) in ayahuasca to pass out of the digestive system and enter the bloodstream.

ß-carbolines have some psychotropic effects on their own. They also inhibit the uptake of serotonin, dopamine, epinephrine, and norepinephrine. These are the body's natural compounds that affect things like mood and other aspects of consciousness.

Combinations

Once you've taken the plunge and tried a psycho-active cocktail, a natural reaction is: 'Mmm, delicious! Can I have another? And does it have to be the same drink, or can I try a different one? The short answer is yes, you can - but do read the 'Dosage Advice' and 'Safety: Plants Beat Drugs' on pacing your consumption; these drinks taste innocuous and can take a while to kick in, making it easy to over-indulge.

Since cocktails are, by definition, mixtures, we should say a few words about the practice of herb combination. Historically, all mind-altering combinations were usually drunk as potions or tonics. From the herbally-fortified wines and beers of antiquity to the ayahuasca teas of the Amazon, synergising effects are at the core of classical psychedelic herbalism.

After 100 years' of dominant scientific medicine, the West is just beginning to rediscover the lost knowledge and skills of the old herbalists (and shamans of today). We're playing super safe and avoiding the use of herbs like opium, henbane, mandrake or any other herb that could be remotely challenging to health.

But while there is nothing intrinsically toxic in any of our cocktails, there are possible psychological factors to consider when combining them. As the authoritative PsychonautWiki warns: "When used in combination with other psychedelics, each substance's physical, cognitive and visual effects intensify and synergize strongly. The synergy between those substances is unpredictable, and for this reason, generally not advised.

The do-not-combine mindset is partly a spill-over from the pharmaceutical research world that demands a scientific-materialist way of thinking about the body and what we put in it. Emphasis is placed on measurability, standardization, repeatability - a framework that makes little sense in the world of herbs. Science tries to single out 'the' chemical that causes the biological effects. In truth, such primary agents typically form part of a family of similar chemicals, like the harmaloids (harmine, harmaline, etc.) responsible for the action of Syrian rue.

Regular consumers of mushrooms/truffles or cannabis may find mixing them to be an enjoyable experience thanks to their synergistic effects. But being comfortable with both substances is crucial to allowing them to facilitate and enhance your experience. If you are not comfortable with consuming either, then ingesting them both at the same time is not recommended; mixing them can increase the chances of an adverse reaction such as anxiety, confusion or psychosis.

That said, cannabis' calming effects can soften the come-up of a mushroom trip, keeping you more relaxed during the early stages of the high. While consuming cannabis can lead to a more intense peak, it can keep you more relaxed during the come-down phase. What can we say? Herbs are paradoxical.

Syrian rue temporarily blocks the body's breakdown of tryptamines such as dopamine and serotonin, as well as psilocybin. It will enhance the effects dramatically; our rule-of-thumb is that a 3g dose taken an hour before drinking a psilocybin drink doubles that drink's potency - so reduce your truffle dose accordingly (unless it's precisely this step-up that you want). Syrian rue will similarly enhance the effects of an LSA seed cocktail dramatically, making it more ayahuasca-like and less like LSD.

WARNING: DO NOT COMBINE SYRIAN RUE WITH MAOI MEDICINE OR TYRAMINE - CONTAINING FOODS.

Cannabis can also intensify the sensory and cognitive effects of LSA, but also help reduce any residual body load or nausea. And - as with psilocybin - can also reduce anxiety when coming up.

Psilocybin can make the LSA experience more like LSD by increasing the visuals. The dose of psilocybin should be low - just enough to cause stimulation - or it will overpower the LSA.

Kola nut increases the "electric" euphoric feel by blocking the vasoconstriction and bronchial constriction caused by LSA, and increasing the visuals. A pleasant combination, good for socialising and dancing.

Safety: Plants Beat Drugs

Like all good bartenders, ours just want you to have a great time and leave feeling better than when you came in, with the weight of the world lightened a little (and for you to get home safely).

As we note in What's Your Poison, it's the dose that creates the effect, anything can be toxic in incorrect amounts, and even poisons can have medicinal and psychedelic effects.

Nothing we've used is dangerous or toxic, even if they tend to be described as 'drugs'. They all have long histories of safe human use, but very high dosages of anything - even water, chillies, or coffee - can have adverse effects.

So nothing is entirely without risk, and there are always exceptions; we are all genetically different and subject to our individual experiences with food, drinks and drugs. Do your due diligence, take responsibility for your own risk and the comfort of anyone else you are entertaining.

Needless to say - we'll emphasise it anyway: NEVER serve these cocktails to someone unaware that they contain mind-altering substances. Not funny.

Saying No To Drugs

Psychedelics are currently revolutionising our understanding of the mind and shaking up the psychiatric medicine industry, offering new modes of treatment for depression, PTSD and other mental and physical health problems.

The problem for anyone seeking to explore these new uses of psychedelic herbs (actually long-established tools and sacraments of indigenous mental and physical medicine) is that pharmaceuticals and psychedelics, whether herbal or synthetic, don't get on well together. They can work in opposite ways, cancel each other out or even lead to severe adverse reactions.

If you are on a pharmaceutical regimen or schedule, we strongly suggest you seek the advice of experts in both pharmacology and herbalism.

Last Call

Although we are at the final pages of this book, we are nowhere near done. High Cuisine is fast becoming recognised as a unique authority on mind-altering plants as we break ground with our innovative products.

Our Bites cookbook combined haute cuisine with these magical plants, and now we've done it again with cocktails.

We've been busy studying and learning about these spirit plants for some time now while combining them into delicious recipes in both food and drinks.

With the knowledge and support of The Bulldog, we're excited to be able to share this extraordinary journey with you.

Join us on this adventure, and stay tuned for our new bottled drinks, books, TV shows and more to come. Visit our website and social media to keep in the loop.

Cheers!

(left) Bottling of
High Cuisine & The Bulldog's
new line of euphoric drinks

Colophon

For this game-changing cocktail book, the pioneering High Cuisine Team joined forces with the legendary Bulldog (the world's first Dutch coffeeshop). Together they have broken all the cocktail rules by creating cutting-edge, mind-altering, non-alcoholic cocktails that are not only delicious but elevating.

High Cuisine Creators:	Anthony Joseph, Floris Leeuwenberg, Isidoor Roebers, Jules Marshall, Noah Tucker & Stevie O'Neill
Creative Director & Photography —	Floris Leeuwenberg
Text —	Jules Marshall
Art Director & Design —	Stephen O'Neill
Chefs —	Noah Tucker Anthony Joseph
Producer —	Isidoor Roebers
Editor —	Rose Casella
Illustrator —	Mathilde Richard
Project Coordinator —	Greg Andruszczenko
Mixologists —	Tess Posthumus Joost Jansen Ben Warren Naushad Rahamat
Special Thanks To —	Henk de Vries, Ruby de Vries, Michael de Vries, The Bulldog Team, Kasper van Beek, Whale Agency, Kokopelli Smartshop, Sensi Seeds, Aroma Innovation & Creation, De Tweekoppige Phoenix Distillery, The Hash Marihuana & Hemp Museum

© 2021
Uitgeverij Terra is part of Uitgeverij TerraLannoo bv
P.O. Box 23202
1100 DS Amsterdam
The Netherlands
info@terralannoo.nl
www.terra-publishing.com

 terrapublishing
 terrapublishing

First print, 2021

ISBN 978 90 8989883 8
NUR 447

All rights reserved. No part of this publication may be reproduced and/or made public by means of printing, photocopying, microfilm or by any other means, without the prior written permission of the publisher.

Every effort has been made to acquire permission for the use of photographs in this volume. Any actors we have been unable to locate are requested to contact the publisher and the photographer.